Writer's Manifesto

MAY Words and letters

ASSEMBLE THemselves and collect WiTHouT effort on PAGes and Screens

MAY I Live My Life

JOY·fully and in Between and DuriNG THese Times, learning to Dance WiTH Distractions, Being conscious of THe WAys My WriTiNG Practice Fills My SouL

MAY My Writing

TEACH Me to leAP FORTH and leAD My Words To Be reAD WHen THis serves Me and OTHers

MAY My Writer's HeArt

Be Free of COMPeTiTioN, COMPArisoN or QuesTiNG For Money or recoGnition, and rememBer THAT We All write for everyone

MAY I write My TruTH

and write AuTHentically even AFter Times THAT I MiGHT write FAlsely, Timidly or witH uLterior Motives. MAY I eMBrACe THe CHAllenges As well AS THe Joys of WriTiNG

Three
Rivers
Press

Juicy Pens, Thirsty Paper

GIFTING THE WORLD WITH your words and stories, and creating the time and energy to actually do it

By SARK

Three Rivers Press
New York

Special Thanks to Trisha Marcy "The Dish", Donna, Kathryn, Carrie, to the brilliant Debra Goldstein

Mark McCauslin production wizard
Jennifer O'connor cover design input
Jean Lynch creative copy edits any mistakes mine

permission for story on pages 136 + 137
Granted By Stacey Hoton
Cover input By McNair

Photographs By Andrea Scher
on pages 136, 169, 170, 171 + BACK cover
Photograph Page 155 By Sandy Horn

Edited with verve + elan By Carrie Thornton
Assisted Beautifully By Brandi Bowles+einweg
Thanks to the great Team at Three rivers!

Library of congress cataloging-in-publication data
is available upon request

ISBN 978-0-307-34170-9
Printed in Singapore
10 9 8 7 6 5 4 3 2

First edition

DEDICATED WITH LOVE
TO: Janice Crow
A Gifted writer
and
Gift TO writers

TO:
WITH THE JUICIEST Pen,

THIS BOOK is for anyone WHO wants to write and SHARE WHAT'S in THeir HEART. THIS BOOK is especially for you if you don't write, Quit writing or BOUGHT an expensive journal THAT still HAS Blank pages.

I started writing AS A CHILD, BUT THen wasn't PUBLisHed UntiL I WAS 35 Due to FEAR, PrOCRASTiNATiON, perfectionism and rAMPanT AvoiDance.

YOU PROBABLY KNOW WHAT I MEAN

NOW, I write every DAY and HAVE pUBLished ABovt A BOoK A year since 1990.

WiTH Jvicy Pens, THirsty PAper, leT me sHow you How To NAViGATe THrovGH THe relentless FeArs and DovBTs THAT can STALK vs and Write AnywAy.

We'll use A Good little BoAT

THere will AlwAys Be reAsons not to write

THiS BooK will explAin aud ACKnowledGe THese, and THen we'll Move riGHT To THe writiAG. I Want to reAD your words and Know WHAT you FeeL. THiS BooK will Be your confideut Gvide, non-JvdGmentAl witness and resoundinGly Supportive Friend.

TABlet of contents

We've all heard, "There's a book in everybody." I think that everybody is like a library of books— bulging with stories, experiences and unique perspectives— toppling off the shelf with vibrancy and inspiration.

Some people are like dusty books hiding at the back of the shelf. Other people are gorgeous novels, full of color. Other people are

pure science fiction

I First Began writing AT AGE 7 in Minneapolis, Minnesota, When I informed My parents THAT

THAT went over well

I kept Detailed notes and wrote Descriptions of our FAMily VACATions THAT Mostly consisted of me writing very carefully, over and over, "I HATE THis Trip, I really HATE This Trip..." THen even smaller

"i HATE MY parents, i HATE MY Brother"

My writing GAined More DiMension When My GrandFATHer Asked me To write about our VACATions in More DETAIL and THen reAD WHAT I'd written To HiM, When I returned.

NOW, I BECAME A "reporter" on our FAMILY VACATIONS, and CHRoNicLeD THe ADventures of our FAMILY: My simultaneously snoring parents, OBSTreperous OLDer BroTHer and BAD MoTeL Furniture. I Developed Microscopic vision and Could SpenD THe DAY AT THe MoTeL, FinDiNG FAScinATiNG THiNGs to write About — LiKe THe STAiNeD plAiD Furniture, IArGe deAD BUGs FLoATiNG Upside down in THe pooL, and THe ScowLiNG Front Desk ATtenDant who looked Up eACH Time I SlAMMeD THe DooR To THe Front office and SHouTed; "WHAT! Do you want NOW?!"

He WAS A reALly CrABBy Guy But I LiKed How MAD He Got and sometimes slAMMed THe DooR ON PURPoSE

One of our more interesting vacations

WHeN I wasn't writing, I was reading, and I developed a voluminous and even voracious book appetite propelled lrgely By my First-Grade teacher who gave out prizes for numbers of Books read. I read a Book a Day For a year and won a clock.

i was so proud of the clock

9

LATER I Began reading shelf by shelf in the library and could almost always be found "WITH MY nose in A BOOK."

I always laughed at this description

sometimes my nose disappeared

By the 5TH Grade, books and writing filled my days and nights and I learned to develop false illnesses so I could stay home from school, to read and also listen to a creative writing program each afternoon. I'd discovered this program on the radio, and it was a miracle for me. I FELT convinced from listening to it, THAT I WAS really a writer.

I often missed weeks of school, one year I missed 92 DAYS.

I ALSO want to SHAre THAT writing and reADing BecAMe an IMAGinATive WorLD THAT I lived in to escApe MY AbvSive OLDer BroTHer and pArents wHo were in DeniAl ABovt it.

MVCH lATer, we leArned THAT He HAD Been Abvsed too and I'M GlAD to SAY THAT I've ForGiven All involved

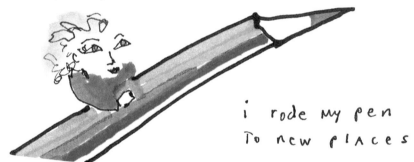

i rode my pen
To new plAces

I literally vsed writing To write myself inTo A DiFFerent reALity, and in Some WAYS, it worked. Writing leD me to THerApy and lATer, AFter MVCH HeALinG I HAD MAny More HeALing tools in ADDition to Writing.

I MOVED to San Francisco in 1982 and Declared Myself to Be An Artist and writer, and Began Living The Life I HAD Dreamed ABout for so long. I didn't HAVe MOney, But I HAD A lot of creative energy and started vsing THAT every DAy to invent New ways to Live while writing.

I BArtered My ARtwork for rent, and went to The liBrary for Free entertainment, Carrying STACKS of BOOKS BACK and ForTH in My purple BACKPACK.

I stAyed up niGHTS writing and DrAwing ABout My experiences and Beliefs, DeliBerAtely seekinG ADventures To write ABout

THAT Summer, I Dropped off A
tAll stACK of DrAwinGS AT THe offices
of THe locAL newspAper to see if THey
COVld Be pUBLiSHed.

i'd Been rejected So MAny times, I
didnt expect MUCH

I THen Went to BiG Sur
To See THe Home of one of My
WritinG Mentors, Henry Miller.
I'd reAD everyTHinG Hed writHen,
GULpinG in His self-reveALinG words
ABout Freedom and SeeKinG,
and THe ABsolute WONDer anD
DeSpAir in Life, and How
WritinG HAD SAved His Life.

and I FeLt So
strongly THAT it
HAD SAved Mine

well, it WASnt
reAlly THis TAll,
But it FeLt
THAT WAy!

WHen I returned Home From Big Sur,
THe newspAper sAid THey'd Like to puBLisH
One of My DrAwings eAcH week and THis
GAVe some crediBiLity to my DreAm of
"Being puBLisHed."

even THOUGH THe pay was $25
per DrAwing

I went Home and Filled More JournAL
PAGes wiTH copious notes ABout BOOKS I
wanted to write. I knew I HAD A lot of
Life to sHAre, I just Felt terrified and
sHy ABout sHAring it.

so sHy

Instead of Actually writing Books,
I continued to write in my JournAls
everyDAy, Hoping to uncover More of
My own stories and write THose.

I WAS Feeling Fulfilled, BUT ALSO scared. WHAT if no one read WHAT I wrote? WHAT if I couldn't Articulate All THAT I Dreamed About SHAring? It seemed MUCH SAFer to JUST write privAtely.

BUT THe words KepT Knocking AND My Dream of PUBLISHing My writing didn't Go Away—in FACT it GoT More vivid and Detailed.

For instance, I wrote A long Description in My Journal of THe Kind of place wHere I envisioned writing THe BOOKS I'd Dreamed of, and it WAS A CottAGe on A Hill in San Francisco.

15

ON A WALK AT 3 AM ONE NIGHT, I FOUND A SCRAP OF PAPER ON A WINDOW OUTSIDE OF A CORNER STORE ON TOP OF A HILL IN San Francisco. It READ:

MAGIC COTTAGE
for A very
SPECIAL person
SMALL. $500

I peered THROUGH A Hole in THE FENCE and SAW THIS tiny COTTAGE, SURROUNDED BY GIANT FERNS, THE FRONT DOOR COVERED WITH IVY. It looked EXACTLY LIKE WHAT I'd DESCRIBED IN MY JOURNAL. I COULD "see" MYSELF THROUGH THE WINDOW, WRITING BOOKS. It WAS PERFECT. I HAD NO MONEY for THE RENT, So I SOLD EVERYTHING I OWNED, BORROWED MONEY and TOLD THE landlord I HAD to HAVE THIS "MAGIC COTTAGE" BECAUSE I NEEDED to WRITE MY BOOKS THERE.

NOW, I WAS REALLY FACED WITH MY DREAM of ACTUALLY WRITING THE BOOKS I'd TALKED ABOUT for So MANY YEARS.

FiRST WHen I WAs in My cottAGe I slept A lot,
ATe rows of cookies, aud wrote really lArGe in
My JourNAL: HOW DAre I write
WHAT I THinK and FeeL?

And, THen in smaller letters: WHo wouLD reAD it?

THen I Got A BLACK Kitten NAMed
Jupiter and stArted DreAminG

sPecifically ABouT How My First BooK wouLD looK,
and WHicH Pen I wouLD Use to write it wiTH, and
CouLD I reAlly Do it?

It soon FeLt liKe THe WAlls of THe cottAGe
were literally BULGiNG witH creAtivity.
I stArted tApinG PAGes of My JourNALs onTo
THe WALls. eAcH DAY, Jupiter wouLD staud on
His HinD LeGs and PeeL THe PAGes off THe WAll
WHere THey wouLD FAll witH A SWOOSHinG
SouNd onto THe Floor and wAKe me up.

One of these pages was called "How To Be an Artist." It was my colorfully written statement that we are all Artists of Life.

I took this crooked, colorfull page to a store in San Francisco. They also had a catalog, and agreed to publish a photo of the poster once to see if anybody liked it. The orders Flooded in and I ended up making 11,000 By Hand. There are now over 1 Million Artist posters in print

Right at the point that I couldn't imagine making another poster By Hand, a publisher who had seen the poster, called about publishing it and wondered why I wasn't writing Books.
Yes. Why wasn't I?

AND I BEGAN THAT NIGHT, BY THE LIGHT of DOZENS of CANDLES, to FINALLY PUT ON PAPER WHAT WAS in MY HEART. RIGHT ALONG WITH MY WRITING CAME MY TYPICAL FEARS— THE NOISE of inner critics, need for perfection and DOUBTS ABOUT MY TALENT crowded in.

THESE FEARS HAD kept me silent and scared for so long and not SHARING MY writing. Now I FELT Determined to write no MAtter WHAT THE FEARS "SAID."

THIS opened A Geyser of creative energy THAT HAD Been Blocked for so long. I wrote My First Book very Quickly— in 2 weeks— and NAMed it "A creative Companion." THE BOOK WAS entirely Hand-printed and Filled WITH Color and ART. THE BOOK did not look Like OTHer BOOKS, But it Sure looked Like me.

WHEN I SHYLY SHOWED THE BOOK TO THE PUBLISHER, I TOLD THEM THAT it needed to stAy crooked looking, and They responded:

"We need to publish This exactly As it is!"

HoorAy!

THis GlowinG little BOOK went out into The world and did exActly As I'd AlwAys envisioned; touching and transforming people. I FeLt THrilled and FulFilled.

I promptly stArted work on My next BooK cAlled "Inspiration Sandwich" WHICH sAys "eAt THis BooK" on THe cover. i loved writing THis BOOK.

I beGan Getting piles of extrAordinAry MAil from All over The world—people writing to sAy THAT THe BOOKS HAD touched THeir HEARTS.

A Few people wrote to sAy THAT THey THouGHT The BOOKS were Messy, unreAListic, and NAive. I leArned HOW TO HOLD BOTH KINDS of responses LiGHTly.

20

My writing continued as I lived a rich, adventurous, highly examined life. On one of my miracle walks, I saw these words etched into the sidewalk, "Succulence is powerful," and I realized how true this was. In that instant, I named myself:

Succulent Wild Woman

I'd been keeping notes about myself and my life as a woman for many years, but hadn't dared share them with anyone. I felt too succulent and too wild and was certain that I'd sound crazy or just "too much" for anyone to understand. I felt terrified to share such personal, intimate details with the world and maybe even more scared of my mom reading it.

She laughed when I asked her if the book was "too much," and she told me she was the original succulent wild woman.

HA!

WHEN Succulent WILD WOMƏN WAS PUBLISHED in 1997, I THOUGHT I'd lose most of my readers who HAD reAD ABout my MAGIC COTTAGE and my WATCHING SNAILS. HOW Were THey Going to respond to my writing About ViBRATors aND "THE Good GirLfrieud MUST Die?"

THE response WAS OVerWHELMINGLY positive, and THE BOOK BECAME A NATIONAL Bestseller, optioned for A Movie, aud translated into OTHer lanGUAGes.

succulence is powerful

THousauds of succuleut women formed Groups All Over THE worLD, aud succuleut WILD Men Joined in too.

I FELT SO profoundly LiBeRATed From All my FEARS of BeING seen for WHO I really WAS, and WHAT I really THOUGHT and Felt AS A WOMaN. It's Been one of THe Most HeALING and creatively inspiring experiences of my Life.

For Me, WRiTiNG is LiKe GiViNG A GiaNT letter To THe WORLD—THe BOOK CONtains THOse letters, and people respond. BY THe resfonses, I AM inspired FurTHer to SHAre my experiences and write WHAT I KNOW. THROVGH My WRITING, I leARn more ABOuT WHO I AM and How I THink.

i'M often FouND writiNG ABOuT LiViNG, PerHAPS even More THaN LiViNG! ALTHOVGH THAT's RAPidly CHaNGING

I THINK THAT MaNy WRiters Are A SoMetimes QUirky, secretive, CRABBy BUNCH— MYSelf especially incWded— and I WOULDN'T enjoy Life nearly AS MUCH WiTHOVT reADiNG, wriTiNG and storytelliNG. I'd Like to welcome you into THe someTimes CRABBy BUT ALTerNATely CURiouS, FrieNdly, inspiring GrouP Called

writers + soMetimes we write iN THe MArGiNs

23

A Quote to inspire you

"Writing only leads to more writing"
Colette

CHAPTER ONE
Being A writer
wings on your pens and fingers

We write for so very many reasons. We write and share our stories because it's fun, it's important and because it changes us from the inside out. and others are changed by our offerings

In a sense, we are all writers of our lives— breathing and living our words.

I think that writing is as easy as breathing— as common and extraordinary as that. Other times, writing is a bit like steering an elephant— there's a lot there, and it might take some time to change direction. Sometimes, writing is like cleaning a submarine with a toothbrush— lots of surface to cover; small tool to work with, but what a sense of accomplishment when finished!

tired little toothbrush

I THINK we Also write to know THAT we Are not "THe only ones" THinking and Feeling WHAT We do. We Discover and interpret THE worLD, and PerHAps Live LiFe More richly and rarely- Because of THe writing.

I write and SHAre sTories to experience Life More THan once. In THe writing and telling of My sTories, oTHers reAD, Listen and respond to me and My words.

MOst of All, I write Because of THe JOY it creAtes. Writing creAtes Connections and MAGic and certAin kinds of PerMAnent BLiss. I can write myself in and out of moods and experiences, and creAte new places to Live in my mind. It's kind of Like POLe VAULting WiTH A pen.

certAin kinds of PerMAnent BLiss

27

DO YOU KNOW HOW interesting, powerful and UNUSUAL YOU ARE? Most of US DON'T. WE THINK WE ARE MOSTLY WHAT WE DO, and THAT OTHER people HAVE More interesting Lives or STORIES. I've learned THAT people dont necessarily recognize THE importance and value of THEir own STORIES. They Dismiss THE FAMILIAR and forget THAT everyone's STORIES HAve power.

we forget

Writing can change THAT. It can show us How incandescent, BRAVE, wise or HUMAN we Are.

writing Helps us remember

It STARTS with your First BREATH and includes All of your experiences including WHAT SCARES you, excites you and Fills you up.

WE HAVE ALL THESE STORIES PACKED inside of us, virtual TREASURE CHESTS JUST WAITING to BE UNPACKED and explored

Treasured CHESTS

28

A Quote to illuminate you

"Fill your paper with
the breathings of your
HEART"
WILLIAM WADSWORTH

MY writing process

My writing process is rather unusual.
I wake up to the sound of birds chirping,
and sunlight floods in as I pick up my
pen and begin to create.
Because I'm so gifted and magical,
The words just flow out like rare honey...
There is no delay, or frustration or
anything that's difficult at all.

W A i T

See next page for real story

30

My Brain contains Many Things:
Habits, Old conditioning, memories
and stories. Sometimes my writing
process looks more like THis:

inside THis writer's brain

don't I need new sponges? Feb 1 was the
chosen day to begin THis book. I did everything
Humanly possible to avoid beginning writing. Then
my neighbor's dog started barking and wouldn't stop, which
naturally caused me to begin compulsively answering
emails until the system crashed and isn't there
SOMETHING else I can clean and WHO or
WHAT can I blame for not writing

YeT

I wonder WHAT's on TV? I wonder
if THe mail came yet. WHAT's THAT
knocking sound?
O Good!
THe phone
is ringing
now...

On THis
particular DAy, I
was searching for ways
To inspire myself, and

31

SO I THOUGHT I WOULD CHECK
MY GUESTBOOK AT planetSARK·com.
Surely THere WOULD Be SomeTHing
encouraging or inspiring THere.

THis is WHAT I FOUND FROM "Jenny"

SARK. I think you are a fake. I've sold all
Your books back to the half price store.

THere WAS A TiME WHen THAT type of
Comment WOULD HAVE Affected me more.
NOW, I LAUGHed and FeLt Grateful
for Her Honesty. and THAT SHe Took THem to A BOOKSTORE
WHere OTHers COULD FiND and enJOY THem
And of course, I know To write
WHen everyTHing is AWFuL or Feels BrOKen.

Write

When you are in despair or euphoria, write it all! Write especially during the sometimes boring middle parts. Write about how pathetic or brave you feel, or how you just saw your unguarded face in the reflection of the TV screen and saw for just an instant... your grandmother's face.

oh dear

Last night I ate a lot of ice cream after dinner and then didn't get much sleep from the caffeine in the chocolate. I could blame not writing on that too. Who can I blame for blaming?

ALWAYS, ALWAYS especially in the first
draft of anything I write, the inner critics
come lurching out of the SHADOWS, jostling
for position. LUCKily they're getting more
ragged now that they're older. I feel a bit
sorry for them — until they start GASPING
and shouting their DisMAY at my "progress"
which is certainly never enough and
WHAT ABOUT THAT reader on your GUESTBOOK
who called you A FAKE?

clearly you are

34

Meanwhile, another Aspect of me
just plain sits or lies down and STARTS
MOVING the pen Across the PAper, and words
Leap out or SNEAK OUT, or Are
pried loose From previously Hidden
places.

WAYS TO MOVE YOUR TOOLS

So HOW DO WE BUILD A place for
"Juicy pens, Thirsty PAper" to Multiply
and expand?
BY MOVING THE TOOLS

Tools searching for their people

Pen and paper or computer keys
and screen. These are the only
tools you need, but tools can only
move when a person is connected
to them.
Lots of good writing occurs in our
minds, and you can happily write that
way all of your life. If you wish to
share that writing with others, you
will need to

M O V E   T H E   T O O L S
Luckily, a lot can happen quickly
when people and tools are moving.

WORDS MULTIPLY

ideas expand

inspiration BUILDS

PAGES STACK UP

THe inner critics sHuffle BACK TO THE SHADOWS
AnD, for THose inclined to Do Deeper work, inner critics Become Allies

read "embracing The inner critic"

SO, WHAT Are SOMe of THe eASiestWAYS
To GeT THOSe TOOLS MOVinG?

PlAY some GAMes
wiTH Yourself

☆ Decide to Give up writinG for THe DAY
and JUST GO TO THe MOVies. THen JUST Before
leAVinG, pick up A pen and MAKe A Quick note
ABOUT WHAT YOU Hope to ACCOMplisH lAter By writinG
THis is A GreAT Trick and often resuLts in severaL Hours of writinG

37

DURING your Allotted "writing Time" START FOOLING Around, DOING oTHer THINGS and THen write A Description of How and WHY you're not writing

This Also often results in several Hours of writing HAppening

Quit writing and don't THink About it. THen CHOOSE To write

This Also often results in several Hours of writing HAppening

Some people can't STOP writing If you Are one of THese people, you MIGHT want to play OPposite GAMES to Get yourself To stop WHen you want to.

WHATever writing process or GAME you engage in, let it HAve HUMOR, HUManity and HOLiness. Most of All, let it Be yours.

Writer's Helpers

As a writer it helps to see things fresh so that we can write fresh. My 3 1/2 year old spiritual Godchild Jonah was in my writing studio, and dumped out all the colorfull paperclips onto the floor. I love when he does this, especially since he also enjoys picking them up. He asked what they were, and I replied "Paperclips." He smiled and said "Paperclicks" and proceeded to attach one to a sheet of paper in a most unusual fashion and hold it up like a flag, chanting "Paperclicking Paperclicking" as the paper flapped and clicked. Now they will always be "Paperclicks" to me, and I look at other objects differently now too.

Jonah sees fresh

39

One of the Best Ways to infuse writing
with fresh energy is to Move Things Around.
Change All The Books in The Bookshelves,
Shake out The Rugs, Light new candles,
Change The positions of furniture.
This literAlly causes new pArts of your
Brain To Be stimulated.
it's Also A GreAT writing Avoider

I AM convinced THAT AT leAST 1/2 of
writing is not ActuAlly writing, BUT
prepAring To write in some FASHion.
Some people Are prone to overprepAre

Ask Friends for Help. Writers
Are often solitAry, and ALTHOUGH Most
writing is Done Alone We can Surround
Ourselves with Friends wHo support
Our writing Life, and ASK for THe
Kind of Help THAT ActuAlly Helps. 40

Ask Friends to:

- remind you that the words are already inside you, you just need to let them out
- ask you to tell them what you love about your current writing
- not ask about your writing at all
- serenade you
- leave you encouraging voicemails

Lists are good for writers, because they're easy to make and create a reason to write at all. Make more lists! Make lists about: who you blame for not writing, books you're going to read, books you'd like to write, people you intend to meet, other writers you admire or are jealous of (or both), writers you just can't stand, make a list of reasons you love writing and put it up on your wall

My friend McNair says, "Gee I love writing every day. Why don't I do it every day?"

we forget how much we like it

So we practice. Create a daily writing practice.

Go to www.dailywriting.net and commit to a daily writing practice

A Quote To remind you

"Begin AT THE beginning and
Go on til you come to THE end
THen stop"

Lewis Carroll

Focused imagination is a form of action

Action
Before
inspiration

Take action and you will surely Be inspired!

Don't "wait to Be inspired"

any action will do, small or large. Tiny works just as well

CHAPTER TWO
Time and Energy to Write + Create
WAYS TO CREATE TIME and energy

BY it's very existence, THIS BOOK will ACT AS A TIME-SHIFTING device, and will Also provide SPACE and EXAMPLES for you to Follow.

MOST of US Are not GoinG to Go on A long retreat To write, and even if we DO, Our REGULAR LiVes WAIT for us to return. THIS BOOK will SHow you How To Fit your writinG into MUCH SMaller SeGMents of Time, and THESE tiny SeGMents will ADD Up to Be Filled PAGes, JOURNALS or BOOKS.

Tiny SEGMENTS OF TiMe = Filled BOOKS and PAGes

My METHODs of shifting Time will
HeLp you Feel Like you HAve plenty,
and To GeT THe words out of your lovely
HEAD GlAD to Her it and onto pAper
W GreAT! P < we will
S O AB V J
solutely All sorts of random THoughTs tumble
Your HEAD is lovely in and out of our lovely HEADs

or screen, NO MATTer WHAT else is
Going on in your Life. I've leArned
How to write and keep writing no
MATTer WHAT THe externAl circumstances Are.
T H e r e will AlwAys Be "A lot Going on" in our Lives
And it is possiBle To write in tandem
WiTH THAT energy and use it to FueL us.
rockeT FueL
I've leArned THAT Literally anyThing can
Be used As A reason "not to write" and THAT
THese choices Are MostLy HABituAL and
Fer-BAsed and can Be cHanGed.

45

I'M Also experienced AT Not writing for long periods of Time, and will show soon WHAT specific lessons I've learned from THAT.

CREATING THE TIME and energy TO Actually write Means THAT ACTION Comes Before inspiration

MANY of us WAit for "THe inspiration" and Only THen TAKE out paper and pen, or turn on THe computer. THis Means THAT we write infreqvently, following GVSTs of inspiration, WHICH Arrive whimsically and less freqvently THan our Action-TAKing energy. I'll show you How to write in New ways Using Accelerated Kinds of energy.
MOST of us prejudge our writing Before it ever GeTs out of our HeADS, CreATing an Unnecessary DelAY. i'll show you easy ways to circumvent THAT, and speed up THe transmission from your BrAin to paper.

YOU'll GO ZOOM

Many of us try to perfect our writing as we go, causing constriction of our creative flow. i will show you how to loosen up

We forget that writing is fun and rewarding, or become convinced that it isn't, and load it up with all sorts of reasons why we can't, or don't do it. We actually think so much about why we aren't writing, that we forget how to use our energy to actually write.
This book will remind you

I spent so many years talking about writing that I actually thought that talking WAS writing. I'd wake up and wonder where the written book was! I've since learned the value of writing in my imagination AND

I've learned how to write in my head and get it onto the paper.

ULTIMATELY, Writing is More Fun Than resistance, once you learn to Access your inspired self, WHO is ALWAYS reApy To write.

By Acting As A Guide, THis Book will demystify Blank white paper or screen, and Give you lots of inspiring starting places and Questions to answer. Your responses will create your new writing template.

Most of All, THis Book will inspire you and show you How to use

Fresh creative energy

THAT you MiGHT HAVe ForGollen you HAVe Access to.

All over THe land, words and ideas TUMBle HAppily onto paper

ADVENTURE

First lots

GOOD idea

yes

Since most writing is done alone, allow this book to act as your "Benevolent witness." It will welcome you each time you visit, and will always listen closely to what you have to say or write.

All of our words and stories are gifts, to and from the world. Gifting the world with your words may mean that you wish to publish your work – or not. This book will explore ways you might wish to share. You might also wish to share your stories and writings in creative community, and this book will describe ways to do that.

49

A QUOTE TO DELIGHT YOU

"When we commit ourselves to writing
for some part of EACH DAY we are
HAPPIER, more enlightened,
Alive, LIGHT HEArted and
Generous to everyone else.
even our HEALTH improves"
BrendA Veland

HOW DARE YOU

Write your words and stories

It's True. It's DARING. preposterous really.

YET if we don't DARE, words and stories will Not GeT written. They'll JVST sit THere, in A lettery clump...

And you'll keep living your life, saying, "I'd like to share my stories and words, but..."

BUT

HOW COULD I really DARE TO PRESUME TO write THAT?

I'll tell you HOW, THE DARING Lives inside THE DOING, and can only be accessed By THE DOING.

THE DARING

So you DO and THEN you DARE

AND A SMILE FORMS

DELIGHT CURLS UP

WAFTS OUT

THE words come out of THEir lettery clump and form THemselves. THey fly onto pages and into BOOKS and THen into

HEARTS
eyes
ears

You Dare

* TO Fill THe WORLD WiTH your enthusiasm, perspective and experiences
* TO BE seen and Known
* TO risk ViBRATiNG AT A HiGHer Frequency
* TO BE reAD By oTHers and judGed
* NOT TO let judGMeut interfere

* TO prActice DetAcHiNG From "WHAT people THink" and turn sQuArely and Fully towards WHAT you THink
* TO BE eMpty and Fill your own well over and over AGAiN
* TO HAVe A writiNG Life!

YOU DARE

* TO DANCE WITH DISTRACTIONS AND invigorate your writing Life

* TO RELEASE yourself From procrastination and perfectionism and write anyway

* TO EMBODY your own story

* TO WRITE THE RAGE AND ordinary and DUMB DetAils

TO WRITE YOUR LIFE

YOU DARE TO DREAM your writing Life into existence.

YOU DARE

* TO BE seen AS FLAWED

YOU DARE

* TO BE viewed and projected upon
AS WILDly successful
and ingenious

* To write yourself open

* TO write THROUGH THE closures
and scars and insecurities and sometimes
LOUD voices THAT repeatedly say:

HOW DARE YOU?

and
answer
just
AS
profoundly

56

This is How I Dare

MAKE iT REAL

FIND A WAY TO LET your words and stories out of your HEAD, DRAWER, COMPUTER or CLOSET and let us SEE and HEAR THEM. WHEN you "MAKE it REAL" it can GLORIOUSLY TRAVEL TO ALL SORTS of places WITHOUT you needing TO BE THERE.

THE VALUE of reADiNG ABoUT WriTiNG

Many writing BOOKS seem to FiND THe GREATEST vAlve in WritiNG itself and not in THe self-reflexive ACT of reADiNG ABoUT writiNG

YeT reADiNG ABout writiNG ActVAlly Allows us To PrActice visVAliziNG WHAT will ActVAlly Be put onto THe PAGe. It stretCHes and exercises our writiNG minds wHen we're not writiNG too.

YOU MAY THiNK ABout A story for A loNG wHile in your HEAD Before puttiNG it "OVT THere." Before it GOes "OUT THere," it spends some AMount of TiMe "in THere."

BOOK CHAIR

Like traveling from an armchair, reading about writing provides a preview of a potential journey. You can see where the other person went, and wonder how you might travel there differently. You can study about where and how the writer stumbled or faltered, and experiment with ways to take your writing journey.

Then, you too can write about all the detours you took getting there and other readers can read you!

YOU MIGHT write at a different pace

· YOU
MUST
READ
A BOOK A
DAY TO
Live Here ·

I once lived in a bookstore in PARIS called SHAKESPEARE & CO. I slept behind a purple velvet curtain Amidst the books. A poster By the book ladder read, "you must read A book a day to live here," and for once, I was Already doing the recommended dose!

I THiNk of BEiNG HuMaN As A kiND of writiNG iNcuBATor. You Are your own

HATCHiNG STATioN

I envision writiNG Novels, cHiLDrens BooKs aND screenplays. Some of THese Are Already in process, some Are in THe HATcHiNG station, GettiNG reaDy to come out.

i dont know wHen

reADiNG is ALSO A Form of exercise for writers. As we reAD, we ABSorB Voices, DetAils, iMAGes

we mAy lAter use

curious objecTs

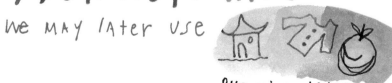
our miNDs lATcH onTo

62

READING is most often A source of GREAT JOY, WHICH Fills wells cells and provides FUEL for our iMAGiNATiON.

I reAD every DAY
I write every DAY

NOT everyone needs to Follow THis scHEDVle, ALTHOUGH THE 2 prActices Definitely complement eAcH OTHer anD Accelerate "proGress."

As you MAY Know, I do not vAlve proGress and process eqvAlly. ProGress iMPlies DestinAtion, wHile process refers to continvous DevelopMent. I THink THAT writing is More About continvous DevelopMent.

A quote to energize you

"I hope you will go out and let stories happen to you, and that you will work them, water them with your blood and tears and your laughter till they bloom, till you yourself burst into bloom."

Clarissa Pinkola Estes

writing as hilarious practice

> There is
> no right or
> good time
> to write.

There are always days that will be easier or more perplexing than others, but really it's all just hilarious practicing. i call it hilarious because it's subject to what life gives and brings us, and that is just so funny and variable

I f you take time to write every day, it will move like a river or the ocean. I appreciate but do not depend on the moments of days or even days where writing flows smoothly. Sometimes it is stagnant, then rushing, perhaps dripping for long stretches of time. Sometimes it stops altogether

65

Being in Attendance for All the
Variations is The ⌐ONLY⌐ PATH.

Sure, you can spend your time Assessing
The Motion and progress of The words,
Discussing your progress or Blocks or
reasons "you didn't write today."
These reasons Are endless and soon
Become LAUGHABLE:

@ The Moon was Full and woke me up.
I Felt Tired today and just HAD
No creative energy To write

@ I realized I needed new towels
and went out To Buy some. By The
Time I Got BACK, it was too late
to write

@ My Friend called and we talked for
Hours. Afterwards, I just wasn't
in The Mood to write

Many reasons for not writing involve A
Story About something you chose to Do Before

66

Writing.

remember THAT ACTION comes Before
inspiration

Writing Likes to Be PriMARY, and
THrives in Focused, concentrated spans of
Time. THese Times dont need to Be
long to Be "ProDuctive."

A Lot of Writing can
Happen in 5 Minutes—1 Hour

"Getting ReADY to Write" can take THe
Most Time:

MAKe A TO DO List   Do THe Dishes
                                    WALK in circles
Get BAtteries   clear A space
    CHECK eMAiL AGAin   Find THe perfect MUsic
  Find Notes   Do A ritual   CAll ——.

67

I DO need some PREPARATION Time to write, But HAVE sHrunk it To Minutes instead of Hours.

MOST TIMES

I put A note on My Computer to remind me Before turninG it on

> HAve you completed some written pAGes?

if THe answer is No, I don't turn on THe computer

MOST TIMES

LOTS of writinG Can HAppily TAKe pLACe WHile WALKinG, TrAVeLinG, WAitinG AT Airports and BeinG on plaues. My Friend KAren and I FreQveutly sHAre our experiences of writinG on Airplanes, and How insvlAted dad cNed for one is WHile on A plane.

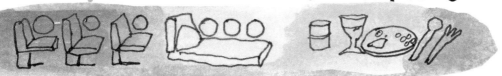

68

I've often THOUGHT of writing A BOOK entirely on planes. My BroTHer andrew claims it MIGHT Be THe BeST WAy for me.

Because THere Are no DisTrActions, and people Bring you THings To eAT and drink

Like Many people, I used to use FooD and sleep As PrimAry writing Avoidance tActics.

NOW THAT I've CHanGed My exercise and eATing HABits, and Sleep THrouGH THe niGHT, THAT doesut work anyMore

SO NOW I HilAriously PrActice writing DAily, and GenerAlly Like How it feels. I've Surrendered to Being A writer (one wHo writes) and Living THAT WAy. NOW it's your turn too!

GeT your self A BiG Juicy pen

and some THirsty pAper

Still, I experience Times of panic, feeling overwhelmed and existential ponderings:

WHY do I write?
WHO's writing?
WHAT is writing?

Also, resisting completing writing can come into play. I'm not sure if I WOULD FiNiSH any writing WiTHout A FiNiSH line. (I won't cAll THem dead lines) "Completion Date" works well too
i WOULD JUST Keep polishing and revising and Adding More THiNGs All THe TiMe

It's All HilArious and I lAUGH often As I practice writing.

CALM
Centered
writer
(sort of)

anxious
worried
writer
(sort of)

SHARING OUR WRITING WITH FRIENDS

I've Discovered THAT SHARING MY Writing WITH A loving and encouraging friend can GREATly ACCeleRATE My inner writing process and Provide A BASis of Support To CAll upon on The DAys when I can only write in "Drips" or not AT All.

Here Are some GOOD THINGS to Know When SHARING WRITING WITH Friends:

@ respect
it MAy Sound oBvious, BUT This is A necessary ingredient for This process. A Friend may respect you, But Does He or sHe respect your writing?

@ conscious Attention
A friend Must Bring THeir conscious Attention To your writing, for it is This type of cwe THAT literally Grows words

⊚ SPACE and time

It is Good if This is not A rushed process, and if There can Be A leisurely Meal or discussion, it can Be even Better

* SMAll AMOUNts of FOCUSed Time Also work if AGreed upon in ADVance

⊚ Allowing True energy

Sometimes when you ASK A Friend to reAD or HeAr your work, it May Become clear THAT something is forced or Mechanical About The process. Allow your Friend THeir own experience of your work.

* Also FEEL Free to conclude THe session if the energy Just isn't THere

⊚ Fill your own well

Give yourself FIRST The Approval, KINDness, enthusiAsm and ADMirATion your work Deserves before showing A Friend your writing. This Keeps THe energy with the work and not your personal needs

◎ reqvest THe TRVTH

Describe WHAT THAT Means or feels Like to you
and [tell] THe TrVTH ABovt WHAT you'd really
Like or need to Hear. Instead of SAYiNG, "I'd
really Like to Hear WHAT you Think, really,"
Give some specific instruction: "I'd Like To
Hear if THe Main CHAracter is Believable to
You, or if you Think This piece is too lonG."

◎ Don't ASK for "constructive criticism"
  if you'd really rATHer not Hear it

        Most of us really don't, or if we
        Do, we need to ASK for and understand
        WHAT it means

◎ Do ASK for WHAT would HeLp you
  and YoUR writinG

    FresH perspective, enTHUSIASM,
    ADMiration or Good energy to ADD to
    your own, or ways your writing could
    Go Deeper or FArTHer

⊚ request and be willing to hear specific types of support with your writing at specific times. educating friends or family about what feels supportive to you, as well as hearing the kind of support they'd want to give, is invaluable

realize that certain friends cannot tell the truth, or may not be able to offer the type of support you're seeking. They may be jealous or just incapable. Learn to recognize if the feedback you receive is "off" or feels false to you. Collect friends you can trust to share your writing with.

My friend JOSHUA came to visit me and I shared page proofs of a new book, and 2 books "in process" with him. His overflowing inspiration and reception of these projects refreshed me creatively in very deep ways. It reinspired me and gave me ideas for new writing.

JOSHVA said later THAT THE visit really inspired HiM too. THis is "compound energy" AT its BesT — we inspire eACH oTHer.

Truly, it was Also an energetic BoosT for me, and I FeLT myself CATApuLTed to New creative levels.

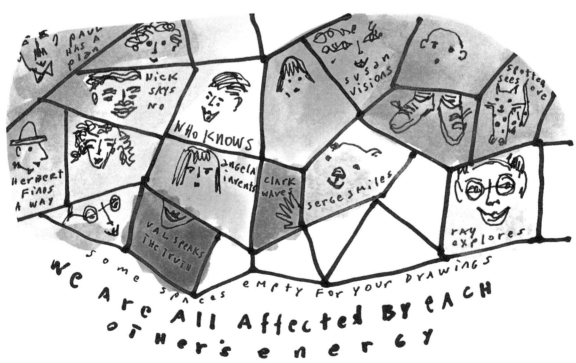

PAUL HAS A PLAN

Nick SAYS NO

WHo KNows

SUSAN visions

SPottee sees ove

Herbert FiNDs A WAY

angela iNvents

CLARK WAveS

serge smiles

VAL speaks THe TruTH

RAY eXplores

some spaces empTy For your Drawings

WE ARE All Affected BY eACH oTHer's e N e r 6 y

75

A Quote to Guide you

"WHAT release to write so THAT one
forgets oneself, forgets one's companion,
forgets where one is or WHAT one is going to
do next, to be drenched in sleep or THE
sea. pencils and pads and curling
Blue sheets alive with letters
heap up on the desk"
Anne Morrow Lindbergh

Your writing inspires others

if you share it, then we can be inspired

CHAPTER THREE
GAMES, STORIES and WAYS TO GET YOUR JUICY PEN MOVING LIKE CRAZY

All ABOUT ACTION

Writing GETS STALLED, DELAYED, PUT ASIDE, FORGOTTEN, OR NEVER STARTED, FOR MANY REASONS, BUT THERE IS ONE PRIMARY FACTOR IN ALL OF THESE REASONS.

THAT THE <u>WRITING</u> PART JUST DOESN'T HAPPEN— ON PAPER OR ON A COMPUTER SCREEN. WE THINK ABOUT, DREAM ABOUT, TALK ABOUT "THE WRITING," AND THEN DON'T PHYSICALLY ACT.

WE GET SCARED

THIS CHAPTER IS ALL ABOUT <u>ACTION</u>. it DOESN'T MATTER FOR RIGHT NOW WHAT you write AS MUCH AS it MATTERS THAT you ARE writing—even if you don't THINK it's "ANY GOOD." ASK your JUDGMENTS TO PLAY IN ANOTHER ROOM FOR AWHILE, AND JOIN ME IN SOME GAMES.

78

MAKE A FAST List of reasons you don't FEEL Like writing
Here's one of Mine:

nothing new to say

no one will read it

I'm Bored

WHAt's the point

I'm tired

I need to Do laundry

It's probably too late to start

now anyway

This loosens you up, Gets you out of your "Thinking only" HEAD and Causes you to write S o m e T H i n G

FAST List of reasons you
don't Feel Like writing

80

MAKE A FAST List of FAVorite THiNGs ABouT A Friend
Here's one of Mine:

She is always HAViNG GARAGE SAles
and complAiNiNG ABouT THem

She swims in THe FreeZiNG CoLD BAy

She HAS Friends THAt Are oLDer THan
90 and sees THem often

She's eccentric and weArs BrigHt Colors

She's reAlly FuNNy and mAkes me
lAuGH reAlly HArd

THis CAuses you to Describe someone FamiliAr, in writiNG

HOW BAD can you GeT?
LeT yourself write someThing reAlly BAD anD BoriNG
Here's one of Mine:

> The school I went to for Junior high WAS reAlly DUMB. I HAted My HAir When I went To THAT school anD My science teACher WAS so stupid He didnt even Know There WAS A Light an A Microscope. AT leAST we never lost A FOOTBAll GAMe.

THis PUTS you PAST YOUr FeAr of writing "BADly"

The next pages consist of
writing "prompts"
   ⊚ PHRASES
   ⊚ descriptions
   ⊚ words
         TO

GROW SOMETHING in YOU

SEE WHAT YOU THINK

SEE WHAT YOU write

UNUSUAL writing DOTS to prompt you
CHOOSE A word or collection of words and write

invisible CLOAK

Clown reunion

Misplaced enthusiasm

Grief lesson

Seeing inside

refusal to move

PACKING

Blank paper

song to your self

RAGGed edges

invented Life

READING LAMP

yes

iMAGinary Friend

FAST Turtle

night of ecstasy

scaled envelope

lost

Tree cLiMBinG

intense request

Conditional love

open door

Travel moment

Aperture at Home

84

uncommon writing prompts
choose a sentence, write a story

You are hurrying down the stairs, carrying a birdcage...

The door cannot be seen from the outside...

Without the book, he couldn't possibly...

As the ship pulled slowly out of port...

It was finished. I knew it, yet...

Before the phone rang...

There were three routes to consider...

After I opened the letter...

Sing to me! I cried...

It was a cluster of butterflies and I...

The more I resisted, I discovered...

BS

Doors to your imagination

These images represent doors to your imagination. Intuitively choose a door and then go to the next page for your instructions

your instructions

1. Call me on the inspiration line 415 546 3742 tell me what you love about writing

2. Go to a park or find some grass. Lie down in complete gratitude

3. Quit Just stop for right now Breathe deeply

4. Imagine your writing sailing free what does it look like?

5. release yourself from anything that doesn't nourish you

6. Ask yourself: what's my most alive choice with my writing?

7. Ignore whatever isn't working

8. Put your writing first see how it feels

9. explore places with your writing that scare you. Write about that

10. How is your splendid life? Write it

11. write or call a writer you admire to let them know

12. investigate your energy style and use the findings to accelerate your writings

13. dive past perceived blocks go deeper

14. invest in yourself as a writer. Get equipment delight in your purchases

15. create your ideal writing environment then make it real

Write your own instruction

87

ⓐ Acronym Game

I Believe THAT Acronyms Are THeir own language and teach curious lessons and cause us to THiNK Differently

My NAMe stands for:

Susan	**S**imple
Ariel	**A**cts
Rainbow or	**R**andom
Kennedy	**K**indness

Try some with your NAMe, friend's NAMe or Book title

Here's A Few About writing:

Writing	**W**e
Runs	**r**ush
into	**i**nto
The	**T**he
envelope	**i**nterior
	now
	Grinning

ⓐ Writing and Dash Game

Spend A DAY, or part of A DAY, writing and DASHiNG

write 2 paragraphs

DASH To THe Grocery Store

write A Page

DASH To THe Movies

write 3 paragraphs

DASH To A NAp

write 2 Pages

DASH To THe Park

Go Deeper, say more

This is a game to encourage you to go further in your writing

My Father was a traveling salesman

My Father missed most of my school activities

My Father traveled weekly for work and used a big brown suitcase and sighed a lot

My Father was a traveling salesman who was home 1 day a week while I was growing up. I learned not to count on him to be there

I used to see all those tags on his suitcase handle and wonder about all the stories he wasn't telling us

I had a traveling boyfriend when I grew up who used to say "I'll be on the road" and I asked him to say something different because I couldn't stand to have another man in my life who wasn't there

What story can you go deeper with, say more about?

STory expander writer's GAMe
To PLAy WiTH oTHers

 ̄I recently played A GReAT version of THis WiTH My PeN Friends Janice and JOHN. We HAD an unexpected Hour TOGeTHer, WAiTiNG For THe Queen MAry To SAiL BeNeATH THe GOLDeN GATe Bridge, and FeLT inspired to create A STory ABOUT WHAT MiGHT Be GoiNG on on THAT SHiP. eACH person HAD 10 Minutes to tell THeir STory, and THen THe next person WOULD ADD to it For 10 minutes. We virtvally "wrote" THe MOST FABULOUS SHORT STORY full of intrigue, romance, comedy, TRAGedy and very cvrious descriptions and CHArActers.

THe CAPTAIN HAD an AFFAIR WiTH THe First MATe and His sister HAD Been SNUCK onBOArd There WAS A SPY NAMed Mrs. BUMBersHOOT and A Missing PASSeNGer WHo WAs Later FoUND To Be one of THe BeATLes

Here Are some oTHer STory expander ideAs TO plAy Jolo:

Before I Moved in, THe people WHo Lived Here were:

_____. I decided not To ever speAK

TO Her AGAin, Because SHe HAD _____.

GeTTiNG on THe plane to _____ Convinced me

TO _____. everyone WHo HAD Gone Here HAD

experienced _____ and _____.

Create your writer's support journal

This is a fun and easy way to support and encourage your writing practice. Use any size paper, punch a hole in the upper left-hand corner, attach with ribbon. Use art or collage for images

o Front cover

YOUR NAME

Writing Accelerator Book

or any title you like

o I love writing because:

o I sometimes hate writing because:

o Writing is fun and easy because:

o I sometimes don't write because:

I've discovered and will use these new solutions:

o MicroMovements are an easy way to complete more writing. Here's one:

o My writer's support network and community consist of:

o Back cover

images and support phrases

91

Interview your future writer self

In this game, you will be traveling to the future and interviewing yourself as a writer. You could also ask a friend to interview you.

Here's an imaginary interview, fill in the blanks. Be as wild, hopeful or simple as you wish. Imagine the title(s) of your book(s) and brainstorm about what kinds of things have happened to you.

It is 2015. Since 2008, when you published _____

_____ _____

WHAT HAS it been like?
When you won _____

_____ and then went to

_____ , _____

Now that your writing is TAUGHT in

_____

_____

How is it for you out in public? What
are they saying about your writing _____
_____
_____

Please tell us about your next work

_____

_____

_____

Being published in _____ languages
must be so exciting. Please describe your
favorite things about it
_____

_____

_____

_____

93

NOW THAT you're A _____ AUTHOR
aud Known for _____ aud _____.
Your DAily Life MUST HAve CHaubed A lot.
PleAse Describe A typicAL DAY or AiGHT in your
writer's Life

_____

_____

_____

_____

_____

isit one of your Books BeiNG MADe into
A _____ ? Tell us More.
WHo's GOiNG to stAr iN THe FiLM ?

_____

_____

94

HOW HAS your writing impacted THe
WORLD? Describe THe MAin WAYS

_____
_____
_____
_____

I SAW you on TV (HEArd you on rADio) BeinG
interviewed By _____. WHAT
WAS THAT Like? Describe your FAvorite
moments

_____
_____

WHAT OTHer writers HAve you Met or Become
Friends with? Tell us

_____
_____

_____

NOW THAT you've published _____ and _____ WHAT OTHER KINDS of writing Are you planning?

_____
_____

_____

Please Know THAT you Are A Mentor or Advisor To OTher writers And Give us your Best wisDom

_____

_____

_____

_____

THANK you! we love you And your work

BOOK TiTle GAMe
WHAT BOOK TiTle(s) DescriBe you?

Here Are 3 THAT sometimes
DescriBe me:

"Susan rushes in"

"Tall, slow vegetarian takes
slow walks"

"you have the right to remain puzzled"

MAKe up A title if you can't find any.
Here Are A few From My weBsight THAT
people Have MADe up:

"Zen and THe Art of MultitAsking"

"Jane Follows Her nose"

"Tired woman sits and Hugs Her Dogs"

"sleepless, unshowered: A journey
into MotherHood"

WHAT Are some titles THAT Describe you?
List THem Here

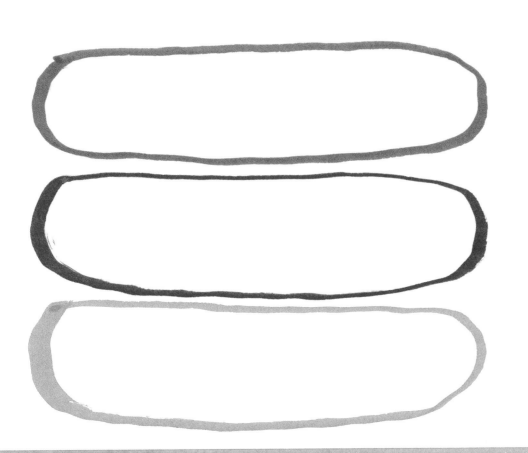

Remember
TO
DeLiGHT Yourself
FirsT
THen, oTHers can
Be TruLy DeLiGHTeD

Your words and stories Are uniquely yours
and can only Be written or described By you.
Before you "show" your writing to anyone,
show it to your self.

A Quote To Direct you

"Writing is nothing more than a
Guided Dream"

Jorge Luis Borges

CHAPTER FOUR

Difficulties, CHALLENGES and WAYS TO Transform These

WHAT's someTiMes HiDeous About writing

Writing can be exAsperATinG, elusive and JusT plAin HArD work. No sAne person sHould AtteMpt it. It rArely turns ouT THe wAY you iMAGine it, you and oTHers judGe it, and it could tAke your wHole life to BecoMe reAlly GooD AT it.

So WHy is writiNG Also so AttrActive? Writing is KinD of like surfinG—it's A CHAllenGe to stAnd up on THe BoArD, But WHen you Do, its A Glorious ride.

In order to sHAre our stories, we need to eiTHer write THeM Down or speAk THem. But for MAny stories, THe writinG pArt cAn cApture WHAt we MiGHt Not Be Able to sAy out loud.

101

THe very ACT of writiNG rewards us even if we never PUBLISH or sHare it WITH anyone. It fills our inspiRATIONAL TauKS and creates someTHiNG TaNGiBle THAT We Can see and reflect upon. It Also GeTs words out of our HeADs and MakeS More space up THere.

MOST of us COULD Use some More space

We All FeAr writiNG BADly. yet we MUST Be williNG To Do THAT in order to practice and write Better. I FeAred writiNG BADly so MUCH THAT I spent AT leAsT 15 yeArs NoT writiNG AT All!

You can set yourself free From THAT Fear By <u>PrActiciNG writiNG</u>.

<u>It's common to underestimATe WHAT it ACtually TAKeS To BeGin writiNG</u>. LeT THis BooK Guide you To BeGin in NeW WAYS

LET'S STACK All of your Fears and
excuses into One pile
and look carefully AT
some, and Briefly AT others,
Before Writing in THe FACe of it All

WHen Fears Are Attended to, it clears
THe way for clear and simple writing THAT
comes From your HeArt.

clear
+
simple

even THe Briefest Attention can MELT FeAr

I invite you to experience THe sometimes
Hideous, often Fulfilling, CHAlleuging and
Surprising PATH called Writing.
Write in THe Direction of WHAT Frightens
or Fills you, and Allow your writing to escort
you into Fulfilling new plAces.

Follow your writing To fulfilling new plAces

every
time
you write
something
valuable
will occur

A quote to invigorate you

"GET BLACK ON WHITE"
Guy de Maupassant

Writer's reinforcements

Every time you write, something valuable will occur

THIS is what we forget. Our minds trick us. Our minds lead us to believe that we can't possibly have anything of value to write about, because we look around and see waves of "Things to Do" and occupy ourselves with these kinds of thoughts

Oil in car not changed

Uncalled Friends

Unwashed Dishes

Disorganized receipts

Overdue library books

lost socks

Due Dates

Children who need immediate Attention

Broken Hot Water Heaters

Writing is power.full and works in Mysterious Ways

writer's WHeeL of SupporT

YoU can Continually remind yourself of oTHer Kinds of supportive THoughts To THink

close your eyes,
put your finger
on The wheel.
LeT THAT phrase
Guide you

Writing Fills My creative SouL

I'M GLAD To SHAre My writing WITH THe World

MY stories HAVE VALUE and energy

iT's A GiFT To Be Able To write + creAte

I BreATHe DeepLy

I can Allow MY writing to FLOW

Writer's WHeeL of SupporT

writing Brings me GreAT JoY

THrouGH writing, new THings Are and uncovered discovered

MY DreAMs Are A MArveLous source of MateriAL

I Know How To provide exquisite self-care and THAT Affects My writing

writing illuminates us From within

Write/Now

writer's solution sheet
WHeN I FeeL or experience:

inertia	I will	M o v e
procrAstinAtion	I will	Do anyTHinG
perfectionism	I will	complete SomeTHinG
inner critics	I will	Give THem New Jobs
Being "too Busy"	I will	rememBer my commitment
Tiredness	I will	re-energize or rest
DiscourAgement	I will	exPand my experiences of encourAgement
Hopelessness	I will	Know it As illusion
Success	I will	use it As memory for Times THAT I dont
Failure	I will	Bless my AwAreness

108

WAYS TO PUT THE SOLUTIONS INTO PRACTICE

WAYS TO MOVE:
* PHYSICALLY MOVE SOMETHING: YOUR BODY, PAPER OR FURNITURE
* CHANGE YOUR ATTITUDE: MOVE THE ENERGY BY CHOOSING DIFFERENT THOUGHTS AND EXPERIENCES
* MOVE FURTHER INTO INERTIA UNTIL YOU'RE TOTALLY BORED

WAYS TO DO ANYTHING:
* Get up. Get out. Get lost
* THE new you will FUEL you
* WALK AROUND MUTTERING, "DO SOMETHING" UNTIL YOU'RE LAUGHING

WAYS TO COMPLETE SOMETHING:
* TINY SOMETHINGS ADD up. Complete 1 5-second TASK
* notice when or HOW you stop SHORT of completion, ASK yourself WHY
* write Down your completions and ADMIRE THEM

WAYS TO GIVE your inner critics new JOBS
* send THEM to another country
* Write THEM A letter FIRING THEM
* CALL A Friend and ASK for HELP reframing WHAT inner critics Are SAYING

WAYS TO re-energize or rest
* Become Horizontal
* Honor rest AS MUCH AS ACTIVITY BY PRACTICING stopping AS MUCH AS STARTING
* express your FEELINGS THROUGH MOVEMENT — This releases energy MAGnificently

WAYS to expand experiences of encouragement:

* Keep a file of encouraging notes or emails. anytime you receive good encouraging words, cut and paste into this file or put in a folder to look at
* Make more posters of encouragement for yourself and put them up on your walls
* Make a list of what encourages you. Cut up the list and put the pieces into a bowl. Draw them out often and read

WAYS to know Hopelessness as illusion:

* "Hopeless" doesn't really exist. It's a story. Go to www.Thework.com
* expand feelings of hope by focusing on what nourishes hope for you, whether it's books, films, friends, music or nature
* rewrite any Hopeless story. Tell it in a whole new way

WAYS to use success as memory for times you don't feel that way:

* Magnify or expand successful moments by writing them down and sharing them
* Put that list somewhere you can find/see it on days when you can use it
* Define and describe what success means for you, then live those successes

WAYS to bless awareness:

* Describe and define what "Failure" means to you
* realize that failure is intrinsically connected to success, and that we must experience both
* To remember what a true blessing every "Failure" is and can be, listen to a song called "Thanksgiving for every wrong move" by Poi Dog pondering

Getting writing onto paper or screen

Most of us are practicing procrastinators, perfectionists and avoiders. We don't have enough time to write, we have short attention spans. We're busy, distracted and occupied with families, jobs and health maintenance. This takes a lot of time!

How can there be any time to write?

There isn't.

You create it. You elbow in, jostle, sneak, trick, play and invent writing time out of moments not hours. You occupy your writing so that it can occupy you.

I invented a method that I use to get writing onto paper. It's called micro-move-ments.

It's so simple that it appears it can't really work effectively. Writers commonly assign themselves huge projects and then get discouraged when it doesn't fit into "real-life."

It's so power-full it's the reason I have 14 published books. Prior to micromovements, I specialized in "talking about writing" to anyone who would listen, until their eyes glazed over.

111

Micro · Move · Ment: 5 sec - 5 min in length

Gentle Date and time written Down: Gentle means Flexible

This creates A "Habit of completion:" your writer's mind will note that something is being Done with your writing

* if you start and 5 minutes isn't enough, just keep Going!

Micro Movement practice

This is for writing A novel. You Fill in the lines Below The samples with your own MicroMovements, or use other paper to practice

Tue 8pm SHArpen 20 pencils

_____

SAT 7pm Meet Friend for teA, Discuss literature

_____

Mon 7 AM turn on computer, title File: novel

_____

Wed 2 pm Move Book PAGes out of Bottom Drawer

_____

Now, you're reADy to GraDuAte to an Accelerated process cAlled The MicroMovement Wheel.

* you can make your own Blank wheel to practice on lAter

Writer's Micro·Move·ment
Wheel of DELIGHT

Here's an example of one

5 sec - 5 Min

Mon @ 5pm
write "THE end" on A piece of PAPer

Fri @ 1pm
locate scraps and notes About My CHiLDren's Book

Mon @ 4pm
Write 3 sentences About WHY I love My kids' Book

realize I'm going to fiLL in THe middle with Microhovements

Sun @ 2pm
Go To CHiLDren's Section AT THE Bookstore For inspiration

write My CHiLDren's BOOK

Thu @ 7AM
FiND My Lucky Pen, Put it next to notebook

SAT @ 3pm
CALL My FrieuD and teLL Her About My CHiLDreus Book

WED @ 9pm
write THe title I now Have on A piece of PAPer, Put it up on THe WALL

Tve @ 8pm
write PAragraph of Description About My CHiLDrens Book

5 sec - 5 Min
5 sec - 5 Min
5 sec - 5 Min
5 sec - 5 Min
5 sec - 5 Min
5 sec - 5 Min
5 sec - 5 Min

I often HAve 10 Wheels Going AT A Time, For 10 Different writing Projects. THAT WAy, each one HAs A Home and is <u>visible</u>, keeping writing out in THe open

113

Writer's Micro.Move.Ment Wheel of Delight

5 sec – 5 Min

5 sec – 5 Min

5 sec – 5 Min

5 sec – 5 Min

5 sec – 5 Min

5 sec – 5 Min

5 sec – 5 Min

5 sec – 5 Min

A QUOTE TO TEACH YOU

"A HUMAN BEING IS NOTHING
BUT A STORY WITH SKIN AROUND IT"
Fred Allen

CHApter Five
THe power of STories
CLAIMING and Writing your Life STories

Even A seemingly tiny story can travel
Great Distances and Deeply Affect other people.
As writers, Most of us can remember How
Hearing or reading A certain story AT THe right moment
Can cause A QUANTUM SHIFT in consciousness.
For instance, WHEN I reAD MAYA ANGeLou's
STories and found out THAT SHe HAD Been Abused
AS A CHILD, I SHIFTed My Life to Accommodate
THe TruTH of My oun Abuse, and resolved to
HEAL, and not Live in SHAMe or secrecy any
longer. Her rAW, truTHful STories led me
to write My oun Books and speak About THe
subject to Groups of people All over THe world.
i WAS HeAled By THis

Years later, I Appeared on A NATioNAL television show with Dr. angelou, to talk About How Her stories and life HAD Helped to Shape and Mentor me, and THen How my stories and Life HAD inspired and Affected oThers. THe producers Asked for people who HAD Been positively Affected By my writing to Be in THe Audience and share THeir stories.

We All Boost each other up

it Felt Like A SHINING circle

THe circle is ALWAYS circLing

writing our stories completes our part of THe circle.

Writing and Claiming your stories is a good way to know that we are not the only ones having human experiences. Through the writing, telling and reading of stories you can find forgiveness, courage, realization and remembering. Through stories, you find out truly that you are not the only one who feels lost, broken, desperate, joy-full, wildly hope-full, yearning or seeking, and best of all, you can reassure others who feel that way too.

I've been writing for over 40 years (including long silences) and publishing books for 18 years. These books are filled with stories, mine and others. I've witnessed the way they affect people and touch their souls. Of course, I've also been greatly touched, moved and inspired by the stories other people share with me. Now it's your turn to share your stories.

i will love to read your stories

118

I'M recommending THAT you Develop A
STORY HABIT if you don't HAve one AlreADy.
By Developing THis story HABit, you will
CreAte A climAte wHere stories will Be DrAwn out
of you and to you, Like MAGnetic DUST. STories
will CHAse you, Follow you, Appear to you
and ASK to Be toLD, SHAred, written Down.

Like Glitter, stories collect and multiply

By writing WHAT you see, Hear or THink, you
literAlly ForM THe Ability to see THe STOries
of your Life More clearly, To explore THeir meanings,
and to use THem As springBoards of creativity.

I've collected so many Gems

Our stories HAve power. Let THis power
Be AT THe HeArt of your writing practice,
and let your writings AwAken and
strenGTHen you in return.

LET All THese sTories inspire you to
Speud your time More RICHLY, and let that richness
Spill onto your pAGes.
Let your stories of CHange and stumblings
illuminate the pATH for THose Hiking BeHind you.
Writing LiGHTs A BriGHT BeAm for All to see, and
THAT LiGHT leads to More Souls SHAring THeir experiences.
Let me Give you A BiG "Juicy pen" and some
"Thirsty pAper" To Drink up your words and sTories.
Let us reAD your stories in THe pAGes of this BOok
                                                  and in
                                            your
                                              Life.

{BiG Juicy pen}

120

A quote to invite you

"I HOPE you will GO OUT and let stories
HAPPEN TO YOU, and THAT you will WORK THEM,
WATER THEM WITH your Blood and tears
and your LAUGHTER till THEY
BLOOM, til you yourself BURST
INTO BLOOM."
CLARISSA PINKOLA ESTES

STORYTIME

HOW did your MOTHER and FATHER meet?
We can answer This question and
tell The "FACTS:" "THey Met Through A
MUTUAL ACQUAINTANCE"

or

We can sHAre THe S T O R Y:
1949

My MOTHer WAS A SAMPle GirL For OLD GoLD CiGArettes. My
FATHer worked in THe CIGAr DiVision oF THAt COMpany.
THe SALes MANAGer, Martin Stampe, Asked My MOTHer:
"WHY Aren't you married yet? In Sweden, WHere
I CAme From, you wOULD Be Considered An OLD MAid
AT 30. You'd Better Hurry up, BecAuse you're not
THAT FAr From 30!"

My MOTHer replied; "I Guess I Just HAven't Met THe
riGHT GUY," and THOUGHT to Herself, "OH DeAr, I Hope He
doesn't try To MAKe me into some KinD of 'Project'"!

123

MARTIN TOLD HER ABOUT ONE OF HIS SALESMEN,
ART KENNEDY. MY MOTHER TOLD HIM SHE HAD
Already MET HiM and didn't THinK MUCH of HiM.
Martin replied;
"Well, you don't HAVE to MARRY THE GUY —
JUST GO OUT WITH HiM!"

    MARtin went STRAiGHT to ART Kennedy and SAid,

"I THiNK you SHOULD GO OUT WITH
Marjorie anderson."
ART replied THAT He didn't HAVE THE Money TO
TAKE Her out, so Martin loaned HiM THE money.

    THE next week, MARTin Asked
HiM HOW THE DATE went, and ART
confessed THAT He HADn't called
Her, and THAT He'd spent THE
Money on SomeTHing else.

MY DAD WAS A RASCAL

124

Martin said, "Now, if you don't ask her out, I won't put up any of your sales racks, and I'll block your orders too."

Reluctantly, Art asked Marjorie to go out on a date.

I remember being so fascinated the first time I heard this story, and leaning forward excitedly to ask my mom,

"Well, what happened?"

My mother replied, smiling,

"We went out for 4 or 5 nights in a row, and had such a good time. We laughed so much and really enjoyed each other. Martin asked me how it was going, and by that time your father and I had discussed getting engaged. We told Martin we'd see him on Thursday, and planned to surprise him with our happy news.

Well, we did see him on THURSDAY—
AT his FUNERAL. He HAD DiED of A HEART
ATTACK AFTER GeTTing US TOGETHER."
This story is precious to me BECAUSE I
wouldn't exist without This MAN NAMED
MARTIN STAMPE, in Minneapolis over 50 years
AGo, BriBing My FATHER and encouraging
My Mother. He HAS BECOME A CHARACTER
in my story too.

A STORY CAN Be toLD and retoLD and
still affect others. A STORY CAN Become
richer and More textured over time.

It CAN Also reveal tidbits THAT
weren't there at The First telling. My Mother
told me years later THAT if SHe HAD Known
AT THE TiME THAT MARTIN HAD BriBed and

THreATened My FATHer, SHe never WOULD HAVe Gone out with Him.

SO Here Are My DEAr pArents:

MArjorie And ARTHur Dec 28 1949

WHAT you can learn from stories

Writing stories is fun and can be practiced by reading other's stories and responding. Creative expression is contagious and loves company.

I wanted to share the story of my parents' meeting, because it is far more interesting than the facts.

Stories Are written.

FACTS are merely recorded. Stories keep the delicious details alive, give flavor to the facts.

Here's what I learned in writing the story of my parents' meeting:

- That relationships are mysterious
- My father needed to be bribed to date my mother
- That "angels" in human form come to help us
- My dad was a rebel
- My mom was feisty and brave
- every love story is unique
- Humor lives on long after an event has taken place
- There are creative ways to meet a partner

128

Writing This story and others

teaches me to listen with my "writer's ear" and be able to use my "writer's voice" to write the story and go beyond the facts. My "writer's ear" collects details, nuance and emotion, and my "writer's voice" puts it down on paper.

"writer's ear and writer's voice make magic"

How have I incorporated this story into my life?

I Believe in serendipity

I trust there are definitely angels in human form and I exist because of one!

I know that sometimes what begins in a "shaky fashion" can turn into something marvelous.

I'm learning that "control" is not always of value

A CHAIR
IS JUST
A BUNCH
of STICKS
until it's formed

LET ME ASK YOU, HOW DID YOUR
PARENTS (or 2 significant people in your life)
MEET?

130

WHAT DID you learn From/About This meeting?

A quote To fulfill you

"THe universe is made up of
STories, not AToms"

Muriel Rukeyser

WHITE BEAR LAKE
"THE COTTAGE"

EACH SUMMER

"AT THE LAKE," THE SMALL WHITE DRESSER STOOD, THE DRAWERS PACKED TOO FULL WITH OLD TABLECLOTHS, CHECKERED NAPKINS, AND THOSE little PLASTIC HOLDERS for CORN-ON-THE-COB.

MY AUNT RUTH HAD PAINTED FOLK ART FLORAL DESIGNS ON THE DRESSER, AND WHEN I PADDED INTO THE BACK BEDROOM, BARE FEET DRIPPING WITH LAKE WATER, THE SIGHT OF THAT little DRESSER ALWAYS CHEERED ME.

THERE WAS A reliABLE "lAKE SMELL" inside THOSE DRAWERS TOO— A MIXTURE OF MILDEW, CEDAR and closed-up-FoR-THE-wiater scent. I USED to rush to open A DRAWER, just to inhAle it.

YEARS lATER, MY MOTHER SOLD THE lAKE COTTAGE and HAD an estate sALe. I ASKED WHERE the little wHite DRESSER HAD Gone, and SHe sAid; "OH DEAR. I SOLD it fr $25."

"HOW COULD you DO THAT!" I SHOUTED IN MY self-righteous WAY. I went on to DETAIL WHAT I loved ABOUT THE Dresser. THEN MY MOM TALKED ABOUT HER memories of it, and HOW it used to HOLD BABY CLOTHES, and HOW HER AUNT HAD LAUGHED WITH DELIGHT WHILE PAINTING it.

MY MOM and I TALKED late into THE NIGHT ABOUT ALL THE STORIES IN THE COTTAGE, and THE simple OBJECTS THAT contained THEM.

SEVERAL years lATer, MY MOM and BROTHER were SHOPPING AT THE MALL of AMERICA in MINNESOTA and spotted A SMALL WHITE Dresser in THE WINDOW of an antique store!

It WAS our dear little Dresser. SHE BOUGHT it BACK IMMEDIATELY and took it HOME.

She told me that when she died,
the little dresser with all of its stories,
could come to live with me.
 After my mom died, my brother Andrew
drove a truck across the country with the
little dresser inside.
 Now it rests happily in my living
room. Anytime I want to be "at the lake"
I just open a drawer and the smell
takes me there.

WHAT simple object(s) in your Home
or Life tell A STory? Describe THe OBJecT(s)

Dear SARK, I want to tell you about My GREAT-GrandFATHer's violin.

My FATHer GAVE me A BEAT UP OLD violin THAT HAD Belonged To His GrandFATHer. It was in need of extensive repair and not playAble. I just set it in The corner and ForGot All About it.

Then I read your BOOK about CreAtive Dreams, and reaLized THAT I'd Always wanted to play A stringed instrument and THAT I HAD one sitting in The corner! I used your MicroMovement MeTHod to set THings in motion with tiny steps.

138

I called a violin shop and took it there to see if it could be repaired. The guy in the store showed me a large black stain across the front, and said that when you draw a bow across the strings of a violin, it leaves a powder residue called resin, which eventually works its way into the wood and leaves a mark. He also showed me a spot at the base of the violin where the finish was completely worn off.

It was the spot where my great-grandfather rested his chin when he played. He loved his violin so much and played it so often, that he literally wore the finish off it.

The man in the store offered to remove the stains, but I said no. The "stains" are a personal history, a connection to my family 3 generations ago.

The violin is over 100 years old and once it is repaired, I plan to take lessons. I will play in memory of my great-grandfather.

Tell About A person in your Life who TAUGHT you something even After They were Gone. WHAT DID This person teACH or SHow you?

140

LET YOUR STORIES TUMBLE OUT

EACH PERSON HAS TREASURE CHESTS FULL OF STORIES. LET US HEAR AND READ THEM !

A Quote To refresh you

"Technology is the campfire
Around which we tell our stories"
Laurie Anderson

CHApTer SiX
STories and portrAits
of oTHer inspiriNG writers
in Addition to YOU

I GET SO inspired By oTHer writers and IM sure you Do too. Here Are some of My FAvorites. I CHose writers wHo Are writing and telling sTories in new wAys. MOST Are puBLisHed in VArious Forms, and I Focused on QuesTions we've Been DeALiNG wiTH in THis BOOK.

I invited eACH writer to ADD ArT and HaNdwriting for THeir portrAit, and IM sure you'll Be AS DeLiGHTed AS I AM By THe resULTs.

Brief introductions of The writers

MARNEY MAKRIDAKIS
is A creative Fountain. Her work is
effervescent, Dimensional and A joy to read and see

Brian andreas
is A wise and tender prophet. His
words and Art sing to the soul

Leonie Allan
is A rADiant, Blooming Bouquet of
ARt and words. Her Life and work Just BEAM

Heather Blakey
is A Deep and spiritual creator.
Her work and service Are LUMinous

ilene Cummings
is A rAre Light and Gifted Facilitator
of The inner reALMs. Her words Are
important and Ageless

Tell us WHAT kind of writer you Are, WHAT Do you love writing?

Marney Makridakis
Artellaland.com

Within the course of the day, I am often very lucky to write all kinds of things, criss-crossing across topics and styles. I suppose my favorite kind of writing, though, is what would technically be in the nature of "free-form poetry" or "non-linear prose", or perhaps something in between — where I can be free from rules or standards and logic, and just let wordlets pour down on me so I can play with them.

I often do this kind of creating with my eyes closed, literally, so I'm not looking at the keyboard or my screen, but typing very quickly whatever happens to come through. The process of conscious thought doesn't play a role in this kind of writing; thought stops, decisions stop, time stops. I don't even know what I've written until I open my eyes, and it's like reading someone else's writing, full of surprises (not to mention typos!) But that is what makes it crystal clear to me that it's not ME that is doing the writing, but a force of creativity that is far bigger than any of us. When I am writing from that state, I can't call the work my own. It's definitely my favorite kind of writing.

I also love writing that is combined with art. The inter-play between image and words is a whole universe of its own. My company, Artella, was born out of my obsession for combining words and art in unique ways, and I never grow tire of working with art - either my own or someone else's - when I write.

If I'm writing something "practical", I'll start by brainstorming. One of my favorite rituals is mind-mapping, even if I have an outline ready. I sometimes mind-map with images instead of words. The point is to fill my head with as much relevant fruit as possible. A painting that I did once (right) is the best way I can depict the state I really crave when I begin writing. Mind- mapping gets those kinds of swirls happening!

There have been times in the past when I've used rituals for a particular project to punctuate the process and make it feel more special. BUT I admit, I tend to make the rituals complicated and overly-involved, and then it becomes something that gets in the way of writing.

"Braindance", 16" x 24"

Before writing or creating, what are some of your favorite rituals?

I love writing because:

It's a safe way to have more than one personality...

...and because my writing knows things I don't know.

...and because it's just the ultimate act of creative expression, and anyone can do it, anywhere. No art supplies to buy, no skills to learn that don't come with practice and willingness. It's God's little cracker ack toy that we naturally have all need to create infinitely, indefinitely, indelibly.

...and because my words could help.

The SENSES!

Bringing in all the senses makes ANY kind of writing waaaaay juicy.

I get so inspired when I read non-fiction that feels like it's fiction, or even poetry, because of the level of imagination invoked. I notice that when I respond to a piece of poetic writing, the senses are often involved.

And it's extra-squirt juicy when senses are used unexpectedly - like when we write what the moon smells like, or what music looks like.

Other juicy nuggets: bold imperfection, muses' whispers, a backpack of memories, nature moments, rhyme & wordplay, the right music, and the right person to read the first draft

WHAT'S JUICY TO YOU?

DO you ever Dislike & Feel frustrated By your writing? if so, WHAT KinDs of THinGs HeLp you?

Absolutely, and unfortunately I think it goes with the territory because I've never known anyone who didn't feel this way at some time or other. What helps me most is to change things up — change where I'm writing, what music I'm listening to, the order in which I'm introducing things, the style or voice I'm using. I find that often, when I can have the patience and faith to not give up, and just make a change or two, it turns both me and my writing upside down in the snowglobe so the good ideas can float down again.

I also must emphasize the value of supportive friends who believe in me, who love me AND my writing! I can call on them when I just need a nudge of encouragement. Getting a supportive email or phone call is like sharpening pencils - it unearths the whole *point*. Authentic writing is not about how I feel about what I'm writing - it's about what is happening on the page.

Aaahhh ... anyone writes!

We write to learn things, about ourselves and the world.

We write to share things, from our furrowed brows and our footprints.

We write to ask questions and answer questions. We write when there are too many questions and no questions left.

We write to remember something forever, and to process things so we can forget.

We write because it's *there* — every person, everywhere, has a story.

We write because it feels really good.

WHO writes?

I often wake up with ideas for both writing and art, and when that happens, I feel that something enchanting is at work! I notice that if I think about a project before I go to sleep, that helps the new ideas come via dreamland, BUT the downside to this is that thinking about projects before I sleep can keep me awake! So I try to find a balance.

And daydreaming plays a large part in all of my writing. I think daydreaming is like a third hand that I use to physically make the act of writing happen!

I love how these are combined in one question! It's a great reminder that even though we may not be able to control our dreams, we surely can make ample time for daydreaming so Muses can come play!

Anyone who feels drawn to write, needs to be writing. And as they say in Hawaii, where I live: "Dass It!"

So if you *aren't* writing right now, explore the reasons why not - and then do what you can to chip away at those reasons so that you have a life, environment, and psyche that supports your writing.

If we don't write our words, nobody else will! So let's do what it takes: find the right cheerleaders, join or start a writing group, make clear boundaries with family about writing time, re-arrange priorities to make time to do it, push past the doubts and fears and critics (inner or outer) to make it happen, surround yourself with inspirations.

The page awaits our very next breath! Let's start with blowing kisses of gratitude that we have minds, hearts, bodies, and imaginations that make creative expression possible, write here, write now!

WHAT words of support + encouragement can you SHARE WITH OTHER writers?

I like to write really short things. Stories you can hold in the palm of your hand, like the memory of a perfect day, or a perfect conversation, or a perfect kiss. Perfectly themselves, indescribable in any other way except with all the pieces it took to make them perfect in that exact moment. The kinds of things you hear walking down a busy sidewalk, or a bit of conversation in a restaurant. The kind of things that make your mind run & jump from the dock into the bright summer air. one moment flying, the next moment landing in the water with a marvelous splash

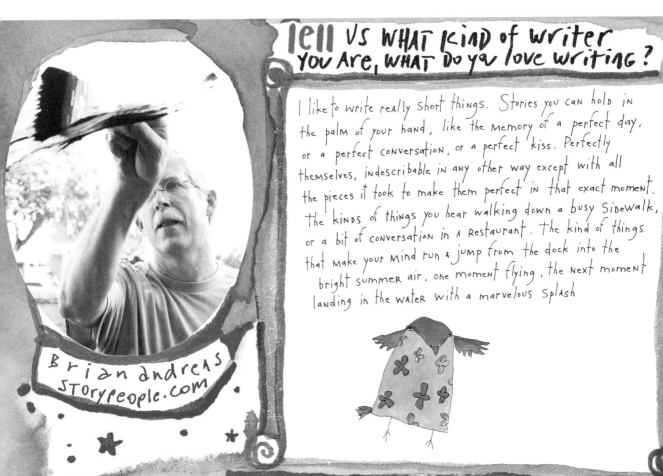

Brian Andreas
StoryPeople.com

Drawing random lines in my sketchbook. I start by holding my drawing pen at the very tip of the eraser end, using only my thumb & forefinger. Then I let the tip drift over the surface of the paper until I have enough lines to remind me of something. At that point, I have the whisper of a beginning & I keep listening until I hear it loud enough to write it down. (Also, it helps if I get up early before anyone else in the house is awake...)

I love writing because:

I love writing because it's a perfect excuse to listen to the world. It's like this: when you sit & listen long enough, many times you can be there at the exact moment something new & beautiful & alive is born. You get to treasure it & name it & hold it up to the sun like one of your own children. It is an immeasurable gift.

WHAT'S JUICY TO YOU?

Love that sees clearly. People standing fearlessly & asking why. Creating a future that works for everyone. Remembering every day that it's all made up & if it's not working, today is the exact day to make it all up again. People doing selfless things. Wine, chocolate & conversations with Ellen.

DO you ever dislike & feel frustrated by your writing? if so, what kinds of things help you?

When I think it's me writing (as in "Look at me. I'm a writer. Would you like my autograph?"), all the time. The thing that helps is for me to have a cup of tea, or go for a walk, or watch a romantic comedy, or draw in my notebook, or wash the dishes. Basically, it helps when I remember that life is in the living, not in the writing. Writers frustrated about writing is an old story & it's something the world can do without. Thank you very much. If it needs to be written, it'll be written. Some day. (Maybe not by me, but that's OK, too.)

The one who made secret treasure maps of his neighborhood & who still sees precious gems in broken glass under street lights. The one who made boats that could fly, out of toothpicks & gamma ray guns out of rubber bands & tape. The one who can levitate for short periods of time & who sees faces in the carpet in hotel lobbies. The one who is still amazed at being alive...

WHO writes?

For me, daydreams & night dreams are all about unfolding from where I've been hunching over my desk & walking out to the very edges of my life, out among the mysteries. The most interesting stuff happens at the edges & not in the center of what I think I know. For the most part, what you think you know is small & safe & quite, quite boring. It's how we keep from being swallowed up by all this luscious chaos.

I'd say just one thing: remember that writing isn't worth anything without a life behind it. Life itself is the secret: the earthy passion & riotous dancing, the wines tasted, the trace of smoky perfume, the lingering glances & the dreams of what may be. That's where the real writing happens. It's in the center of a life lived full out, loving it all. Loving the people & animals & trees & rain & sunshine & then putting it down in a way that you & everyone else never forgets. I wish you all good things in the living that is yours (& it's all good things...)

WHAT words of support + encouragement can you share with other writers?

I am a *Writer* of *Spirit*, documenting *joy* & sharing *wisdom*. I am a Scribe of the Soul, writing the *stories* of our *sacred* & *human* selves. I am a woman with *pen* in hand, seeking the *light*. I want to *ignite* this whole word *alive* with my writing...

leonie Allan
Goddessleonie.com

In writing I find my ♥WINGS.

~ Sometimes I *smudge* myself with burning *sage*... but mostly I find I can put too much *energy* in preparing to *create* - as though I want to have clear energy <u>before</u> I write, forgetting that *writing* <u>is</u> clearing. The best way for me to prepare is to *D♥ IT*. Let the *pen* make love to the paper.

I love writing because:

I come home to myself on paper. ♥ I find the Wise Old Woman who knows the way & will gently lead me there. I find my four year old self who knows how to dream. I find the woman I was meant to be.

WHAT'S JUICY TO YOU?

Women in sacred circles

Paint & ink on my hands...

Seeing the Divine in myself & others...

Being on this Earth is pretty much the most awesome thing ever...

Do you ever dislike & feel frustrated by your writing? if so, WHAT kinds of things help you?

YES. But mostly, the frustration is about THINKING about writing & not actually DOING it. So, my way to drive out of Frustration Funkstown is to.... Write.

(a walk on Mother Earth is also very healing)

DO YOUR NIGHT & DAY DREAMS contribute to your work? How?

Let your words become tiny winged miracles, flying off into the wind to change the World...

WHO writes?

Dreams are imaginings of my highest self. They are visions of possibility. They are reminders of our creative magnificence. Dreams are a part of me & all I do.

SCROLL OF MAGNIFICENCE

Dear You,
This certificate below recognises your qualifications & hereby proclaims you a writer.
Qualification:
You were born.

WHAT words of support + encouragement can you SHARE with OTHER writers?

Tell us WHAT KIND of writer YOU Are, WHAT Do ya love writing?

Like the chrysalis writing is about metamorphis and change. Writing rescued me and transformed me into Enchanteur, a wild, free spirited, celestial, winged creature who presides over Soul Food and ancient Lemuria, land of my dreaming.

An imagineer, a purveyor of creative stimuli, an explorer — these are just some of the incantations writing has made possible. What is there not to love about living a dream?

HEATHER BLAKEY
DAILYwriting.net

Artistic midwife

I don't do rituals! Rituals are a form of procrastination. I tell my students that thinking is dangerous. If I waited until I had my cup of coffee, sweetened with Carnation milk, read my emails, sharpened my pencils, tidied my desk, spread the smoke from sage around my working space, read my daily tarot or waited for Mercury to have a good hair day, nothing would happen at the Soul Food Café. I live by the mythos that I have created on the site. I actually make writing and art a daily practice. Each day I cut out images from magazines, paste them in my visual journal, make narratives on little film strips, draw and write. Sometimes I draw cartoon characters on the top of my finger tips and then have rival gangs communicating. As I visualize my characters being adventurous, visiting faraway places and sucking the marrow out of life with a straw, ideas flow and the writing part just happens.

Before writing or creating, what are some of your **FAVORITE RITUALS**?

I love writing because:

WRITING
R·O·C·K·S
It gets
me going

WHAT'S JUICY TO YOU?

DO you ever Dislike & feel frustrated by your writing? if so, WHAT KINDS OF THINGS HELP you?

DO your night or day dreams contribute to your work? How?

WHO writes?

The Soul Food Café was built as a waterhole, a kind of billabong, manna in what can seem like a cyber desert. It was built to provide creative stimuli for all those people who need a trigger or a prompt to inspire them. For example, if you visit Soul Food's Chocolate Box you can choose a delectable chocolate, immerse yourself in the material and then respond in some way. Soul Food is a playground. It is a place that provides the reader/participant with things to do. It works on the theory that after you have played for awhile you will catch on that writing is not hard if you actually take the time to write about every day things, every day. So if you are stuck today cut out some news headlines and use them, or do what I have done here. Place a character in a scene! Here, I have drawn Sibyl Rivesleigh is in her parlour at the Taverna di Muse in Lemuria. She is preparing for her evening performance at the Taverna. Lord Riversleigh will be utterly askance when he realizes that his daughter is going to wear the skimpy number hanging on the mannequin. But then, from his perspective, Sibyl always behaves outrageously. Life is never dull when she is around.

WHAT words of support + encouragement can you share with other writers?

The Lavender Lace Bra
A Tale of Aging Beautifully

by Ilene Cummings

ilene cummings
THEBEAUTYCONVERSATION.com

I am a compassionate writer because the years have taught me how to see.

I'm an honest writer because I bring parables of hope and deep beauty.

I love writing stories that can teach others.

The stories I know best are from my own life.

I learn so much about myself through the writing!

Because I write about women—I see a group of women in front of me. They do not have to be women who I even know. I feel how deeply I love them and understand them. I honor them completely. I do not "co" them, I shine my light on them. And they respond to my sincere wish for what is in their best interest. They are always a sweet and wondrous audience. They bring out the muse that lives deep inside me. My fingers hook in, and away I go.

I love writing because:

It brings out my well-earned wisdom and my rich beauty.

It brings out the best in me.

It is just so wonderful to feel this.

Writing about loving your body is juicy to me. So is writing about the magic of sex and the ways to be sensual and gorgeous at 76.

Writing about these things always leaves me feeling happy with myself and thanking God that I started on the long path to self-discovery 36 years ago!

WHAT'S JUICY TO YOU?

DO you ever Dislike or feel frustrated by your writing? if so, WHAT kinds of Things Help you?

Reaching out and complaining helps a lot!

This requires venting to another writer who understands the unbelievable things writers go through when they are frustrated, are burned out, and feel that kind of karmic debt is holding them hostage!

Nobody can understand the special kind of suffering that writers can feel at times, except another writer.

A person who feels
a yearning, a destiny, a belief,
or a great knowing.

They have something inside
that wants to be expressed.

It is NOT about celebrity
or money as much as it is about
the soul wanting to be
made visible.

WHO writes?

DO your night or day dreams contribute to your work? How?

A deep love of justice informs
my work. I want to contribute that sense
I have about what is right. I feel deeply
that women are amazing and should be
championed for that. For 30 years
I have conducted seminars for women.
I always see their strength and ability to
love. This seems to be even more true as
we age. It is like a waking dream to see
women, who have done the work,
approach old age with surrender
and good heartedness.

Love yourself—follow your desires—trust your voice—trust what you
know. Sing and dance, but write. And then write some more. No excuses.
I know how you feel. I moved 3,000 miles so that I would be without the
distractions of a big city. I gave up my friends, my work, and my boyfriend.
But it is worth it. Do whatever you have to do in order to write. But, woman,
you owe it to yourself and to the world to make your voice known. Praise
everything, even the years when your resistance to being wonderful kept you
stuck. It is a new day, with a new beginning. You are not alone.
We are all going with you. Write, woman, write.

WHAT words of support + encouragement can you share with other writers?

THIS PAGE
is
dedicATed
to
YOU
As A writer

YOUR pHOTOGRAPH
OR ART HERE
+ NAMe

WHAT Do you love To write and why?

A Quote To excite you

"writing is my form of celebration
and prayer"
Diane Ackerman

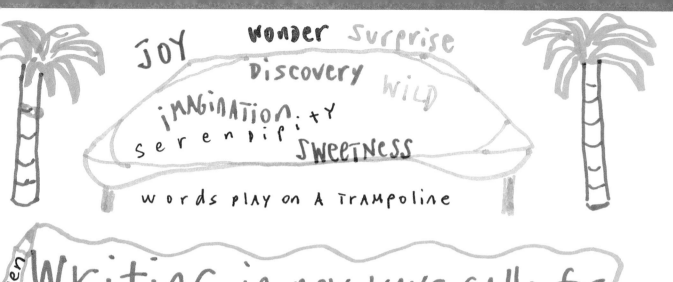

JOY WONDER SURPRISE
DISCOVERY
WILD
IMAGINATION·ITY
SerenDiPiTY
SWEETNESS

words play on a Trampoline

Writing in new ways calls for new tools. Having a JUICY pen can cause words to leap onto the page, and play on a paper trampoline. New colors or fonts can transform your computer.

Thirsty paper needs to drink ink. You'll know when you've found the right kind of notebook or paper when it makes you swoon and begs to be filled up with your writing. I really love writing with purple Pentel pens — they stay really juicy after a long time, even if you leave the cap off. I'm always eager to experiment with new pens too. I am absolutely captivated by paper samples.

162

I like to see and feel how the ink moves on the paper.

New creative tools + toys are fun!

Writing can become a visual journey, using art or collage to add images. You dont have to be a "professional" artist to make writerly art, any more than you have to be a published author to write breathtaking words.

WHAT FILLS YOU UP?
Tell us.

I make thick inspirational "storybooks" using articles from magazines and photographs. Later, I use these to fill myself up creatively and get inspired to write my own words and stories.

Try making one for yourself. There are so many writing and creating tools to choose from and experiment with. Your writing can be transformed by making bold new choices.

play on paper

163

Most people don't experiment with visual tools Because They're scared of How it will look When They're done. WHAT THEY don't realize is, It's more fun to Just Begin and Allow The "mistakes" to inspire you FurTher. I say to Just Dive in, especially if you're feeling shy or uncertain

We Are All DeligHTed By color, and ForgeT To use it lavishly and unsparingly. wHen writing includes colors, it inspires us each Time we look AT WHAT we've created.

JournALs and BLank BOOKS Are inviting containers for our writings. Some of us Feel Hesitant to write in new journaals "Because THey're so nice," But it's really Because we Fear THAT our writing isnt As Good As THe Journal. Are THose Blank pAGes really THAT vALuAble? even if you're nervous, I want you to write anyway, and Fill THose Journal pAGes with writings from your Heart. THese PAGes can Also Be on CLoTH, GlAsS, cement or _____?

CHAPTER SEVEN
PUBLISHING, STYLE, PROCESS
TO THOSE WHO WISH TO BE PUBLISHED

I MOST OFTEN HEAR THIS STATEMENT:
"I'd really like to be published, but I don't have the slightest idea about how to do it."
i used to tell this same story too

If you're someone who currently tells this story, may I offer my hand to you? Let's WALK TOGETHER TO A BEAUTIFULL GARDEN and FIND SOME SOFT EARTH, and DIG A HOLE.

NOW, BURY THIS OLD STORY in this HOLE and COVER it up.

This is an OLD story you dont need anymore.

Let's FIND OUT WHAT THE NEW STORY is.

PUT YOUR OLD STORY IN HERE

Here's the first paragraph of your new story:

> I AM SMART, CAPABLE and KNOW
> WHATever I need to ABOUT PUBLISHING.
> For everything else, I can learn and ASK.

AND THEN DO THE WORK of learning and ASKING!

This work involves stretching and reaching out in new ways and providing a publishing education for yourself.

People often act intimidated with regard to publishing. People relentlessly believe THAT PUBLISHERS don't need or want THEM.

PUBLISHERS (exist) BECAUSE of THE creative input and outpourings THAT come THEir way.

THey Also exist BECAUSE THEY chose to operate A Business and THEY appreciate BOOKS and writers

rePEATING THE OLD Story = reinforcing THE STORY = DOING NOTHING new towards BEING PUBLISHED.

YOU can MAKE new choices ABOUT your writing and PUBLISHING PATH.

Many people use their lack of knowledge about publishing as a reason not to complete a book or piece of writing.

i used this for years

It's convenient to think, "Well, if I don't know how to "Get it out there", I might as well take my time writing it." This often translates to _never_ writing it.

TAKING THE TIME ISN'T THE ISSUE, Choosing to never publish and claiming that there's some publishing system you can't participate in, _is._

Your new story about being published needs to include (YOU) and the ways (you) do things with your writing.

MAKE your writing real

then it can travel without you

Complete enough of your writing to share let go of what others "think"

create a publishing system that works for you and your personality

self-publishing is a great option

ignore anyone who says it can't or won't work

invite them to your booksigning

stop telling an old story about publishing

just write now

write and create for your own satisfaction and joy, not whether or how you publish your creations

167

TO PUBLISH Merely Means to MAKE public.
explore your reAsons for Wanting to SHAre your
writings, and ASK yourself if it's coming More
From your Mind or HEART.
I personally Advocate consulting with your HEART,
Because THen you will Likely creAte THe kind of
writing THAT touches oTHer HEARts.
It is Also of GreAT value to
write and not publisH. PrivAte
writings enjoy A kind of Freedom
THAT published work Does not, and this
Freedom May Fuel your writings in
FundAMentAl ways. you May wish to "Grow"
your writing Before publisHing it.

CArefully Tended writing Grows HEARt Flowers

PUBLisHing does not MAKe your writing Better
or More vALuABle — it is A GiFt and responsibility.
If you wish to Be published, CHoose WHy
and How, and ADventure into it with your
FUll HEART

A Quote to AMUSe you

You can never GeT A cup of teA
lArGe enouGH, or A Book lonG
enouGH, To Suit Me
                    C.S. Lewis

your own writing voice and style

WHAT is your writing style? Do you know? Can you identify your writing "voice?"

If not, begin to practice with your style and voice and study these subjects. You can do this by exploring the resources in chapter 8 of this book, or by a process of self-study.

I receive a lot of mail from people who wonder whether I've somehow written all of the color-full handwritten books, or that my style is much the way they would like to write.

I do understand some of WHAT THEY MEAN, because I've sometimes admired a book SO MUCH, and wondered how I could ever write something as true, or as good.

WHAT I've learned is that their good writing and style absolutely nourishes mine,

JUST AS my Books and style nourish others.

I think it is exceptionally important to realize THAT your written expression, Purely imagined and offered, is yours Alone and cannot Be copied or Duplicated. Your writing style is Also yours, and comparing your writing To others, or Quitting Because you think "it's Already Been Done" is A sure way to stifle your writing.

THere is only <u>one</u> of <u>you</u> Develop your own voice and style, Allow your writing To emerge, Grow, expand, and Be AS (Trve) and AS (you) As you can possibly MAke it.

and THen, let us read it!

HOW SARK BOOKS ARE MADE

I write and create All
of My Books By Hand,
Page By Page.
These pages Are Then
Photographed and printed.
Doesnt THAT Sound eAsy?

It is, and THere Are lots of pARts to it:
I write 4 DRAFts of every Book, WHicH Means
THAT I Handwrite AT least 1,000 pAges fr eAcH Book.

DrAft 1   noBODy sees or reADs But me and THe Moon
DrAft 2   my editor, Ageut and selected reADers Make suggested revisions
Draft 3   I incorporAte 1/2 - 1/3 of THe suggested revisions
DrAft 4   I turn eAcH pAge into A piece of origiNAL ARt

I Get Most inspired By ARt + words TogeTHer,
So I MAKe skeTcH DrAwings As I write, leAving
spAces to Add in FinAL Art later.
I love Being an AUTHor and an ARtist.

I create Hundreds of Drawings and Dozens of Paintings for each book. I also do all of the art for the front and back covers. The final art and production parts of the book require lots of scheduling and focus. There are also copy editing, proofreading and color approval processes. I also do a lot of writing while sleeping, so my dreams are important to my book-making process.

Each book takes about 8-10 months to create. I then tour and promote the book, working closely with the publicity and marketing departments. They're all great, dedicated people

I love EACH of THE 14 BOOKS I've created, and AM Delighted and Honored To HAve written THem.

THey Are created THroUGH me More THan By me

I Also enjoy interacting WITH people who reAD My BOOKS and Like to Discuss THe ideas in THem.

especially moments of serendipity and TransforMation

You can CAll me AT
415·546·3742
It's An "inspiration phone" line

Or come and see me
AT planetSARK·com
I'd love to see and
Hear WHAT you're
Writing ABout and
CreATing in your Life

A quote to open you

"Good writing is a kind of skating which carries off the performer where he would not go"
Ralph Waldo Emerson

excellent writing re·sources
just for you

I've compiled <u>some</u> of my favorite writing inspiration and instruction places, pen and paper supplies, writer's websights, blogs, self-publishing links, organizations, music, writer's retreats, and writing books.

writing inspiration+instruction

because the internet changes frequently, if any of these links are not current, put all kinds of words into search engines. ask just incredible things and receive incredible answers!

nanowrimo.org   write a novel in a month

writingbliss.com   free+fee-based email courses

selfhealingexpressions.com   sandra schubert writing for life

writersweekly.com   writing ezine

storymind.com   novelists + screenwriters articles and classes

halzinabennett.com   writers coach

Writing inspiration
and instruction continued

MAGGIE OMAN SHANNON
THenewstory.com Online salon

DailyWriting.net HEATHER BLAKEY's incredible cove of creativity

Artofstorytellingonline.com COACHING service

poemofquotes.com/tools/ Free elements + tools For HELP with writing

word-wrangler.com LAURIE WAGNER's Writing classes

GeTKnownnow.com/selfHelpBook.html SUZANNE FALTER-BARNS

TheMuseisin.com Jill BADONSKY's inspiring spot

C writersplace.com 52 weeks of writing bliss

JUICY THIRSTY
Pen and Paper supplies

* Be sure to use .net *pen island.net All pens, All the Time

MArcuslink.com/pens/ Glenn's pen PAGE

Handprint.com/HP/WCL/WATER.html World's Finest Guide To Watercolor painting

FlAxART.com COOL creative stuff

Handmade-paper.US/ Handmade papers

Meininger.com GreAt online creative store

ArtellAland.com MARNEY MAKRIDAKIS's AMAZING place for writing, Art, creativity

Creativity-portal.com Chris Dunmire's extravaganza of creativity

17

writer's websights i like
(NOT A comprehensive List)

dannygregory.com

rebeccawalker.com

Alanis.com

leslie-land.com

sabrinawardharrison.com

planetSARK.com

elizabethgilbert.com

MOONLIGHT-CHronicles.com

writer's BLOGS i like
(i think of them as journals)

teawithmcnair.typepad.com/McNair wilson

Jengray.com
Jen Gray

leonielife.com
leonie Allan

superherodesigns.com
audrey scher

gorgeouscuriosity.blogspot.com/
Vanessa Carlisle

myspace.com/
ATOOSASPAGE
ATOOSA.rubenstein

put your blog, or a friend's blog here

creativetimes.blogspot.com/
eleanor Traubman

self-publishing resources

PNAPUBLISHING.com
Dan Poynter

writers-exchange.com
Sandy Cummins

iuniverse.com

Allied with
Barnes + Noble

lulu.com
digital
marketplace
BOB YOUNG

BOOKSURGE.com
part of
AMAZON

Artellaland.com
Marney Makridakis
Her e Books are
truly outstanding

writeand
publishyour
Book.com
+
Businesswordsmiths.com
Sid Smith

Selfpublishing.com
Ron Pramschufer

i Am truly excited About
Self-publishing and Digital
Opportunities

Writer's Organizations

ASJA.ORG American Society of Journalists + Authors

PW.ORG Poets + Writers

AUTHORSGUILD.ORG

Music for Writers

Just 3 of my favorites, all listened to while writing this book!

JOSHUAKADISON.com

KARENDRUCKER.com

GABRIELLEROTH.com

Writer's Retreats + Advances

HEDGEBROOK.ORG
Widbey Island
near Seattle
Washington

HOLLYHOCK.CA
Cortes Island
British Columbia

OMEGA.ORG
Rhinebeck
New York

FINDHORN.ORG
Scotland

KRIPALU.ORG
Berkshires
Western Massachusetts

ESALEN.ORG
Big Sur
California

MIRAVALresort.com
Tucson
Arizona

ARTISTSHELPING
Artists.ORG
California

STARWAE.com
Sonoma
California

180

inspiring BOOKS For writers

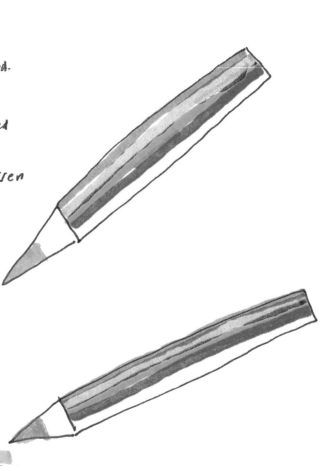

SOUND of PAPER
JULIA CAMERON

WRITING BEGINS WITH THE BREATH
LARAINE HERRING

WRITE: 10 DAYS TO overcome writer's Block. period.
KAREN E. PETERSON

THE WRITE TYPE: Discover your true writer's
identity, and create a customized
KAREN E. PETERSON   writing plan

THE BOOK THAT CHANGED MY LIFE
edited by ROXANNE J. COADY + JOY JOHANNESSEN

THE WRITING LIFE
ELLEN GILCHRIST

SO YOU WANT TO WRITE
MARGE PIERCY and IRA WOOD

WRITING FROM THE HEART
NANCY SLONIM ARONIE

WRITING THE WAVE
ELIZABETH AYRES

WRITE IT DOWN, MAKE IT HAPPEN
Henriette Anne KLAUSER

THE PRACTICAL WRITER
edited By THERESE EIBEN and MARY GANNON

More inspiring books

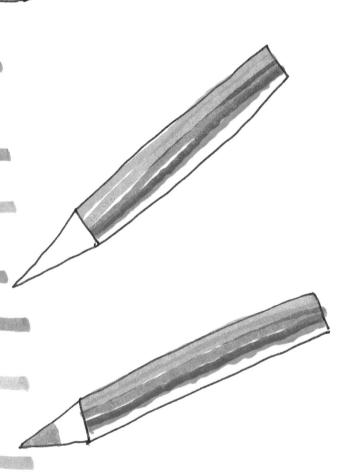

Zen and The Art of Writing
Ray Bradbury

The Right To write
Julia Cameron

Writing Down The Bones
Natalie Goldberg

Writing As A Way of Healing
Louise DeSalvo

Writing Alone and With Others
Pat Schneider

Writing From Life
Susan Wittig Albert Ph.D.

Like Shaking Hands With God
Kurt Vonnegut + Lee Stringer

Courage and Craft
Barbara Abercrombie

The Faith of A Writer
Joyce Carol Oates

Write Away
Elizabeth George

Writing The Fire!
Gail Sher

Still More inspiring Books

The Art of Fiction
  Ayn Rand

I Give you my word
  Janice crow

If you want to write
  Brenda Veland

writing in A convertible with The Top Down
Christi Killien and Sheila Bender

Writing PAST DARK
  Bonnie Friedman

your corner of The universe
  Audrea Campbell

writing on Both sides of The Brain
  Henriette anne Klauser

writing Toward Home
  Georgia Heard

All SARK Books, especially
Living Juicy, SARK's New Creative companion
MAKE your creative Dreams Real, SARK3 Journal
                    and play! Book

reading and writing
  robertson Davies

How A Book is MAde
  ALiKi

To All My Juicy Friends i Thank you, i Love you

Brice + John

Andrew + Otto

Bill Hubner

VALI CINK + JONAH

emily claire

PAULA D'NCY

To All the PAST friends + new ones

Craig McNair Wilson

Steve + Elaine Musick

Zoe Arielle

YOFE + DAVid

The island Big Island HAWAii

Clissa, Charlie, Alex

West Judy Roberts

VanessaCarlisle

KAren + JOHN

EAST HAMPton

SUSAN REAGAN

Goody Cable

MARNEY + TONY + peanut

Kevin + Serge

Jennifer + PAOLO Gianluca, Alessandro

Amber

SHAnnon + Jose

STARWAE Sonoma

leslie, GAVin, Savilla + Christian

Suzanne + Spotted

round lake wisconsin

Andrea, MATT + Ben

JOSHUA KADISON

SABrina WArd HARrison

eleanor TRAVBMAN

edie, meredith Claiborne

esalen + Big Sur

DEBBie edwArds

ATDOSA rubenstein

robin + JOHN

Virginia Bell

LUCHINA, DAVID Giles, LVC

Robyn posin

ilene cvmmings

Jan + Marina

JUneAU ALASKA

PATRICIA

Katie Grant

Bill + MAY-REE

ray DAVi

Mike, Michelle + SAMAntha

KATHryn + AJA

Joe Brown

JASon + ericA

Merrell

cheri Huber

THANKS TO THESE OUTSTANDING PROFESSIONALS

Kevin Rhodes
Irving Bernstein + Arvind Shenoy
Steve Musick + Destiny Caith
Debra Goldstein + The Creative Culture
Donna Gunter + Eva Potter
Trisha Marcy
Carol Zimmerman
Kristine Hicks, Elizabeth McDowell, Cliff Solomon
Murney Makridakis
Theresa Nelson, Chris Bergstedt at Nelson + Nelson

Gary Rosenthal

TO MY DEAR NEIGHBORS

Jimmie + Marti Spot + Bella

Sally

Michael

John + Lea

Ted + Candace

Brad + Linda

Jim + Lyse + Charlie

JM + Melissa + Buster

THANKS TO MY PUBLISHERS + PRODUCT PARTNERS

Three Rivers Press
Simon + Schuster
Celestial Arts / Ten Speed Press
Hay House
Amber Lotus
Independent Bookstores + libraries
Every person buying a book or product
All previous product partners
To all the new product partners

OTHER BOOKS BY SARK

VISIT ME AT
PLANETSARK.COM